TAROT

THE STAR

TAROT

HOW·TO·READ·THE·FUTURE

FRED GETTINGS

CHANCELLOR PRESS

First published in Great Britain in 1973 by the
Hamlyn Publishing Group Limited, under the
title *The Book of Tarot*

This edition published in 1993 by Chancellor Press
an imprint of Reed Consumer Books Limited
Michelin House, 81 Fulham Road, London SW3 6RB
and Auckland, Melbourne, Singapore and Toronto

© Trewin Copplestone 1973

ISBN 1 85152 251 4

A CIP catalogue record for this book is available
at the British Library

Printed in China

La Lune.

1. The cartomancer Madame Nicole, using nineteenth century cards, of both the Major and Minor set.

2. 'The Fool' of the Major Arcana, based on an eighteenth century design.

3. 'The Devil' from the same design.

1

6

Introduction

The Tarot pack is a set of cards which may be used either for divination, or as a philosophical machine for answering almost any kind of question put to it through a medium or someone familiar with its powerful symbolism. The pack consists of two quite different, though not entirely unrelated, groups of cards, totalling 78 in number: 22 form the Major Arcana, and consist of mysterious and alluring images of a deep esoteric content (figure 2); the remaining 56 closely resemble the picture and pip cards of an ordinary set of playing cards (figure 12). There are very many different Tarot designs, most of dubious authenticity and quality, the merits and demerits of which will be touched upon in a special section: for the moment it is sufficient to note that the set examined most completely in this present book is well over 250 years old, and was printed in France, but is almost certainly of much earlier Italian origin.

As a technique for looking into the future, the Tarot set offers possibilities not contained in other predictive methods. It is virtually unique in that anyone may learn to use it after only a few weeks of study, augmented by a little experience; though of course, as with all arts, many years of study and practice are necessary before full proficiency may be attained. Compared for example with the complex predictive techniques of its nearest oriental equivalent, the *I Ching*, which takes many years in the mastering, as well as a high degree of mediumship, the method of the Tarot is easy to handle as a predictive tool. Indeed, the most important single practical virtue of the Tarot is that it offers excellent opportunities to those who do not have the time or inclination to study occult matters deeply, but who nevertheless wish to acquire a working technique by which special symbols may be manipulated, with a view to contacting the subconcious levels within the self. It may be objected that a method which is easily acquired may not be as valid as one which takes years to master; there may be an element of truth in this, but the real point is that the Tarot has a field of application different from that of most other predictive techniques. The essential difference between the Tarot and, say, astrology as instruments of divination is more than merely one of convenience; it is also a question of scope. Once a person has learned sufficient of the complex doctrine of astrology, it is possible for him to use a horoscope figure as the basis for answering very many questions about the chart's subject, and it is quite possible for him to assess the whole personality and life structure of that subject. The more easily

THE FOOL

2

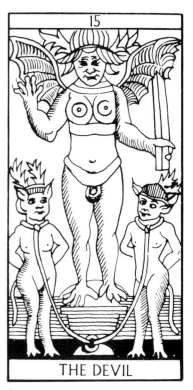

THE DEVIL

3

7

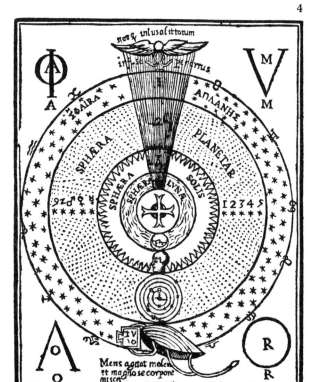

4

5

learned method of Tarot divination does not have such a wide application: it is generally possible to answer thoroughly only one question at a time with these cards, though theoretically at least there is no limit to the number of questions which may be posed in sequence. Astrology requires only one basic horoscope for each querent, no matter how many questions about himself that person may put, while the Tarot requires one basic pattern of cards in response to each question asked by each person. It is extremely unlikely that anyone would be able to interpret horoscopes usefully and accurately without at least three or four years' careful study of astrology: on the other hand, it is possible to learn how to operate the Tarot cards after only a few weeks' study and practice.

The Tarot cards may be used for other purposes than foretelling the future and answering questions – there is, for example, a game of Tarot – but the cards are generally applied exclusively to these two purposes. It is with this in mind that the following explanatory text has been designed, with a view to presenting some of the most exciting philosophical concepts connected with the cards as instruments of divination, on a level which may be applied practically in everyday life. Naturally, my experience and prejudices have limited the scope of the study: for example, particular emphasis is laid upon the 22 Major cards of the Tarot pack, as I feel that these alone should be used for prediction – not only because the size of the pack makes for ease of handling, and because the symbols are extremely deep in their import, but also because the historical indications are that these were intended originally for the purposes of divination, while the larger pack was in all probability designed as an ordinary card game. Again, in the section on the 'formal pattern', which is the card order studied for a response to questions (figure 258), I concentrate on that method which I myself have found in practice to work in the most satisfactory way, even though I am of course aware of the existence of very many different formal patterns, as well as of variations upon my own well-tried method.

It is widely recognized by diviners and occultists that the Tarot cards always give a pertinent response to the question, and, indeed, that it usually offers a little more than was bargained for. When a response to a question regarding past, present or future is required from the Tarot pack, the diviner, or someone familiar with the Tarot pack, will set out a series of cards, laying them out in the 'formal pattern', using the Minor or Major Arcana, or a combination of both, depending upon which method he himself favours for interpretation. From this formal pattern he will then proceed to study the forces and impediments which the cards represent, and by applying these to the context of the question, produce an answer satisfactory to the querent. Although the Tarot method works, it must be admitted from the outset that no one has ever been able to explain *how* it works. Most diviners refer the matter to the intervention of spiritual agencies, to geomantic earth spirits and the like; the more psychologically-minded refer the matter to the workings of the intuition or the subconscious. Both viewpoints are tenable and reasonable, providing we are prepared to admit that we do not understand the intuition or the subconscious any more than we understand spirits.

It does not appear to be very important whether the intuition or the spirits operate the cards: there remains the strange fact that through the formal pattern of cards it is possible to reach into the future, and by so doing to help others at times of crisis. It is only a matter of personal judgement as to what refinements of interpretation are allowed to spring from the intuitive mind or 'attendant spirits' of the cartomancer, or as to what influence the fears, prejudices and aspirations of the querent himself will have on the interpretation. One short anecdote from the history of prediction will serve to illustrate several considerations underlying cartomancy, and thus enable us to catch something of the philosophy of prediction through the Tarot.

Henry Cuffe, the scholar and author who was secretary to the Earl of Essex towards the end of the sixteenth century, consulted a cartomancer about his future. He was told that he faced a somewhat unpleasant and untimely death. Cuffe required the diviner to show him exactly how he would meet his fate, and he was told to draw out three cards entirely at random from the Tarot pack. He placed the cards face down on the table as instructed by the diviner, 'who then told him if he desired to see the sum of his bad fortunes, to take up these cards. Cuffe, as he was prescribed, took up the first card, and looking on it saw the portrait of himself *cap-à-pie*, having men compassing about with bills and halberds; then he took up the second, and there he saw the judge that sat upon him, and looking up the last card, he saw Tyburn, the place of his execution, and the hangman, at which he laughed heartily; but many years after, being condemned for treason, he remembered and declared this prediction.' Cuffe was hanged at Tyburn on 13 March, 1601, for his

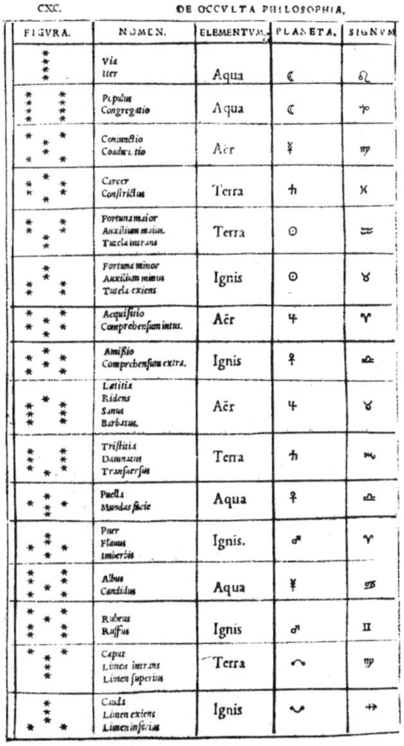

FIGVRA.	NOMEN.	ELEMENTVM.	PLANETA.	SIGNVM
	Via / Iter	Aqua	☽	♌
	Populus / Congregatio	Aqua	☽	♋
	Conjunctio / Coadunatio	Aër	☿	♍
	Carcer / Constrictus	Terra	♄	♑
	Fortuna maior / Auxilium maius / Tutela intrans	Terra	☉	♒
	Fortuna minor / Auxilium minus / Tutela exiens	Ignis	☉	♉
	Acquisitio / Comprehensum intus	Aër	♃	♐
	Amissio / Comprehensum extra	Ignis	♀	♎
	Laetitia / Ridens / Sanus / Barbatus	Aër	♃	♉
	Tristitia / Damnatus / Transfixus	Terra	♄	♏
	Puella / Mundus facie	Aqua	♀	♎
	Puer / Flavus / Imberbis	Ignis.	♂	♈
	Albus / Candidus	Aqua	☿	♋
	Rubeus / Rufus	Ignis	♂	♊
	Caput / Linen intrans / Linen superius	Terra	☊	♍
	Cauda / Linen exiens / Linen inferius	Ignis	☋	♐

4. *A sixteenth century diagram showing the microcosm and macrocosm relationship, upon which astrology is based.*

5. *Casting a horoscope from a set of ephemerides and tables of houses.*

6. *The sixteenth geomantic figures used for predicting the future.*

7. *Consulting the Chinese philosophical text, the I Ching, in order to study the future.*

*8. Mary, Queen of Scots,
Attributed to Ondry.*

*9. The execution of Mary,
Queen of Scots in 1587.*

9

part in abetting the Earl of Essex in his treason.

Apocryphal or not, the story serves to illustrate the workings of the intuition both in the diviner and in the querent. We must presume that the first card was the Traitor (a version of The Devil in Italian packs), the second card was the Justice, and the third was the Hanging Man. From these cards it would have been very possible to read several variant stories, rather than the one which Cuffe read instantly: another reason, for example, might have seen the story of the downfall of Essex, with Cuffe as a sort of dumb but guiltless witness. The point behind the story is that the psychological propensity itself translated the cards, for it was Cuffe's own self-knowledge – his awareness of his guilt or potential guilt – which induced him to read so much in the three cards. Bacon, in the official Declaration of the Treason of 1601, described Cuffe as being 'of a turbulent and mutinous spirit against all superiors', whilst Coke, the Attorney General and prosecuting counsel, dubbed him 'the arrantest traitor that ever came to the bar'.

Another possibility, which is not so far-fetched as it might seem, is that there was something in Cuffe which already knew about his past and future life course, and that this something was not normally available to his normal stream of consciousness: the presence of the Tarot cards, or of the medium himself, may have lifted Cuffe into a higher stream of awareness. Those diviners and mediums who have tried to rationalize their activities have talked of trying to allow their subconscious mind to take predominance over their conscious mind, in order to let it envelop the subconscious mind of the subject. They attempt to do this because they believe that the ego, overself, subconscious mind (call it what you will) of their querent knows the past and future which has been arranged for the body and mind it controls.

The story of Cuffe is recorded here because it is the story of us all. We each read into the pattern of cards our own selves – our forebodings, our patterns of thought, our inclinations, and perhaps even our subconscious knowledge of what is actually going to happen to us. A case in point is the water speed champion Donald Campbell, who 'read' his own death in a group of ordinary playing cards the night before his last fateful trip on Lake Coniston. His 'conscious reason' for such a forceful interpretation was that Mary Queen of Scots had drawn the identical cards on the night prior to her execution. In such forms of divination the symbols on the cards, our own memory traces, and our own inner knowledge, combine to sharpen the usual dullness of our perceptual apparatus: the cards bear some resemblance to a highly refined Rorschach test in which the formless ink blots have been replaced by archetypal images which help the hidden truth in the spirit to reveal itself.

There can be no denying that the work of prediction is very much the work of intuition, yet the further we push into the unexplored realms of prediction, the more we are faced with our own ignorance, and the more we are compelled to admit that we do not understand this magic.

In the ordinary way, that is to say in an ordinary state of consciousness, man is not able to make contact with the world of his subconscious – nor can he see the world as it really is. He must see the world through what Maupassant called 'the ridiculously imperfect instruments' of his ordinary perceptual apparatus. In this way the world is perceived as a manifestly confused and contradictory arrangement of apparently chance happenings and situations. In his ordinary state of awareness man cannot escape this level of reality. However, all the esoteric religions of the world teach that this realm of 'meaningless illusion' to which man is committed is merely the phenomenal manifestation of a unified noumenal world which may be made directly apprehensible to man. The Tarot pack is one of the 'philosophical machines' which have been bequeathed to ordinary man towards this great end of learning about life by permitting a brief escape into a spiritual domain where past and future are gathered. In its methods that Tarot resembles all great divinatory techniques, such as the Chinese *I Ching*, which uses sticks; the Arabic *Geomancy*, using stones; and the ancient, world-wide astrological systems, which use complex symbols and numbers. In technique, however, the Tarot remains splendidly isolated, by virtue of its intrinsic simplicity as a divinatory method. This by no means implies that the cards themselves are simple, for they are in fact extremely complex as graphic symbols: as a pack of designs, the composite pagan and Christian forms, the sure traces of esoteric knowledge, the fragments of teachings, the pregnant symbols, glyphs and graphic structures constantly bewilder the historian and surprise the diviner, yet never fail to enchant the layman.

10. Donald Campbell in 1963.

11. Donald Campbell, in his attempt to break the world water speed record, in 1967, somersaults in his 'Bluebird' at more than 300 m.p.h., and is killed.

11

12. The two of swords from a nineteenth century Minor set.

13. 'The Chariot', 'The Justice' and 'The Hermit' from an Italian Major Arcana.

14. Six cards from the same Italian set of Major cards.

15. 'The Lady Pope' based on an eighteenth century card.

16. 'The Hermit'. The Significance of the individual cards depends upon their relationship to the others.

IL CARRO

LA GIUSTIZIA

L'EREMITA

RUOTA DELLA FORT

LA FORZA

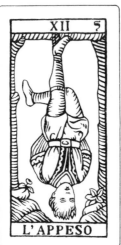

L'APPESO

IL SOLE

IL GIUDIZIO

IL MONDO

12

14

The Major Arcana

The 22 important Tarot cards which are known as the Major Arcana, or *atouts*, consist of strange emblematic pictures, mainly of mediaeval origin, containing both pagan and Christian associations (figure 213). In popular cartomancy it is generally assumed that each card has one or perhaps two fixed interpretations, but this is not so: each card is capable of an almost bewildering number of interpretations, though each of these meanings emerges in an orderly fashion from the structure of the card itself. There are at least five levels of meaning contained within each card, the first being linked with the graphic structure hidden within the form of the card, the second with individual symbols portrayed, the third with the distribution of colours, the fourth with the traditional associations attached to the cards, and the fifth to the distinctive 'feeling' which each of the cards engenders in its complete form. Because of this it is impossible to say that each card has one particular meaning: indeed, each of the Major *atouts* has many substrata of meanings, though all connecting with one or other of the five levels within the card. It is this peculiar richness of imagery and stratification of meaning which makes the 22 cards so versatile, so adaptable, so sensitive in responding to a wide range of questions.

It is possible, and indeed even necessary at the beginning, to examine the cards individually in order to study their meaning, but it must be understood that they are ultimately to be considered in groups, in formal patterns, activating with their symbolism a group 'meaning' which escapes the limitations of the individual symbols of the cards. In this connexion, it must be seen that the meanings of the cards are amended considerably when they are united in a sequence of formal order, and at the same time the interpreter of the formal order must consciously change the meaning, and adapt the symbols, to accommodate the framework of the question which gave rise to the specific formal order. We may examine the principle of such changes in an extremely simple example. If we place the second *atout*, the Lady Pope (figure 15), which is obviously a female card, next to the ninth *atout*, as in figure 16, we may, even without a knowledge of the symbolism of these cards, see that thus they represent a man who has found a woman, presumably after a long search. The age of the man, or indeed the difference of ages between the couple, needs only arise if it is implicit in the question in some form. The man is holding up a lamp, facing the woman, who is looking away rather than at her book. The woman is seated, the man moving (however slowly), suggesting that it is

THE LADY POPE

15

THE HERMIT

16

13

THE HERMIT   THE LADY POPE

the man who is taking the initiative, though the woman, by looking at him and being distracted from her book, is not entirely disinterested. Depending upon the nature of the question which gave rise to such an arrangement of cards, the diviner would introduce the question of age, or the difference between the two in spiritual terms, or the fact that the man is world-weary, or a wanderer, and so on, but the general assumption that a new relationship is being established could not be denied from this order of cards. Now, if these two cards are transposed, quite a different relationship is established, and the meanings of the cards fundamentally changed.

The Hermit is now moving slowly away from the woman, suggesting a parting, which has left the woman reasonably happy (for she is seated comfortably), but which has left the man in a state of loss, for he is world-weary and searching for something, presumably for his lost love. One gets the feeling that she is distracted from her book by the memories of the man: perhaps she is musing on the relationship, but this has undesirably come to an end, and has particularly affected the man. From such an elementary example of the meaning-structure which cards may together establish, the beginner may be able to see something of the rich promise of interpretation which these remarkable cards offer.

Only 21 of the Major cards have numbers attached to them; the final one in the series, sometimes called the Zero Card, is the unnumbered Fool. The thirteenth card, an image of Death, has no name in the English and French packs. The complete set of 22 cards are named as follows in the English, French and Italian packs at figure 19 opposite.

Within my own favoured system of divination (see page 129 ff) it is necessary only to know something of the symbolic background of these Major cards in order to make satisfactory interpretation of formal patterns, as the Minor pack is not used at all. Certain systems of divination including all 78 cards are in use, and are discussed in the appropriate place.

The following observations on the symbolism of the Major Arcana are not meant to be an authoritative final statement of the nature of the cards, but rather notes which will open up lines of thought for the reader himself to pursue, allowing him to develop a rich set of associations for each card, and thus facilitate his interpretation of formal patterns obtained in response to questions. Cartomancy is too personal a thing for anyone to be precise or dogmatic in his interpretation of any one card or group of

	ENGLISH	FRENCH	ITALIAN
1	The Juggler	Le Bateleur	Il Bagatto
2	The Lady Pope	La Papesse	La Papessa
3	The Empress	L'Imperatrice	La'Imperatrice
4	The Emperor	L'Empereur	L'Imperatore
5	The Pope	Le Pape	Il Papa
6	The Lovers	L'Amoureaux	L'Amore
7	The Chariot	Le Chariot	La Carozza
8	The Justice	La Justice	La Guistizia
9	The Hermit	L'Hermite	L'Eremita
10	The Wheel of Fortune	La Roue de Fortune	La Ruota
11	Strength	La Force	La Forza
12	The Hanging Man	Le Pendu	L'Impicato
13	(Untitled image		La Morte
14	Temperance	La Temperance	La Temperanza
15	The Devil	Le Diable	Il Diavolo
16	The House of God	Le Maison Dieu	La Torre
17	The Star	L'étoile	Le Stelle
18	The Moon	La Lune	La Luna
19	The Sun	Le Soleil	Il Sole
20	The Judgement	Le Jugement	Il Guidizio
21	The World	Le Monde	Il Mondo
0	The Fool	Le Mat	Il Pazzo

cards, and it has therefore been my aim to avoid being too didactic. With this in mind I have attempted to explain certain recurring symbols, on each of the levels already described, with the aim of indicating possible lines of thought to which each card may give rise. In order to avoid undue repetition, and in order to leave fields for the reader to exercise his own judgement, I have made certain omissions: for example, although I trace certain of the basic symbolic forms in terms of colour and graphic elements, I do not refer to them specifically where they are clearly recurrent. For example, the underlying structure of the Hanging Man (figure 20) is clearly reversed in the World (figure 21), and whilst I touch upon the importance of the reversal, I do not consider it necessary to discuss a second time the fundamental structure of the cross and the triangle, these having been dealt with in the section on the Hanging Man.

In particular I have emphasized the astrological background to certain of these cards, where I have felt this is useful in understanding their meanings. This is necessary because, though all writers on the Tarot are eager to affirm the close connexion between the signs of the zodiac and the *atouts*, there is much confusion as to what precisely is meant. For example, there is little agreement between authorities as to which card is linked with which sign, and the general confusion suggests that very few 'authorities' on the Tarot are also authorities on astrology, which is far from being a superficial subject. My commentaries on the twelve important zodiac cards are meant to remedy this.

Another correction I have attempted to make to the almost 'traditional' failings in the study of these cards is in relation to their 'esoteric' content. All authorities and adepts affirm that the cards are secret devices and contain hidden meanings, yet in their books they rarely explain what these meanings are. Almost all books on the Tarot may be grouped into those which are prolix and well beyond understanding; and those which are disappointing in their simplicity, for what they offer is superficial, and it is evident that the Tarot cards themselves are far from superficial. Symbols of the quality of the Tarot work on many levels, but in order to demonstrate at least one level of esotericism within the pack, I have concentrated where possible on an analysis of the underlying graphic significance of the cards – a significance which alone accounts for many of the apparent distortions in the pictures – distortions which have been 'corrected' by such 'authorities' as Waite (compare the plate 25 with Waite's version at

17. 'The Hermit'.

18. 'The Lady Pope', now looking towards the departing Hermit.

19. The most common English, French and Italian names for the Major cards.

20. 'The Hanging Man', symbol of man unregenerate.

21. 'The World', symbol of regenerate man, is in almost every respect the graphic opposite of the previous card.

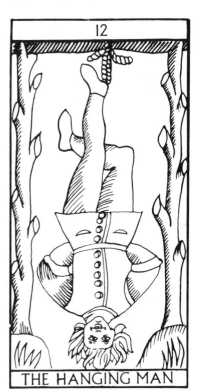

THE HANGING MAN

20

THE WORLD

21

22. *'The Juggler'*.

23. *'The Hermit'*.

24. *'The Fool'. These three cards have in common the stick held in the left hand of the person depicted. The stick is a symbol of materiality.*

25. *'The Juggler', based on an eighteenth century card.*

26. *'The Magician', designed by Waite (see bibliography) in the nineteenth century.*

27. *'The Moon'.*

28. *'The Sun'. These two cards are based on an eighteenth century design.*

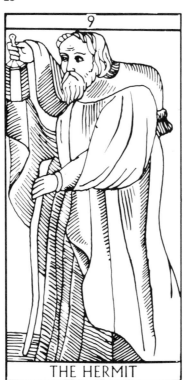

THE HERMIT

THE JUGGLER

THE FOOL

plate 26, for example), who more often than not failed to grasp the real meaning of the cards on a deep level.

It must be understood that these cards are intended to be springboards for intuitive judgements, rather than happy hunting grounds for scholars of esotericism. Over and above the individual structures and symbols of each card there is the very important 'feeling' the image produces – compare, for example, the feelings engendered by the Sun (figure 28) and the Moon (figure 27) – and these direct emotions must remain the final touchstone for good divinatory judgement. This is the one very excellent reason why one must be calm, if not spiritually attuned, when consulting the cards, for correct intuitive judgements rarely spring from a mind in turmoil (see page 130).

The symbolism of the cards is very rich, and it is certain that their full meaning can never be fully grasped by one person. It is not uncommon for someone to be inwardly moved by the symbolism of the cards at first acquaintance, for although the conscious mind cannot readily perceive their deeper meaning, the real significance is often readily accessible to the subconscious levels. The cards are, so to speak, the alphabet of the emotions, and because they deal with emotions and are intended to convey understanding on an emotional plane, they are by their very nature not capable of being invested with a fixed verbal interpretation. The symbolism of each card exists on several levels, and the level upon which they are interpreted will depend wholly upon the medium or diviner. A response to a question cannot be more 'philosophical' than the medium who is directing the operations, for this is one form of divination in which the spiritual, mental and emotional levels of the medium cannot normally be transcended.

The following analysis of the Major *atouts* is based on the Tarot form as it has been preserved in the so-called Marseille Pack, with occasional reference to the Italian Varallo pack, which differs from the French in a few significant details. The reasons for this choice will be evident to anyone who studies the section on the history of the Tarot at page 139. The differences between these two packs is really a matter of what may be called 'direct symbolism', as contained in the immediately obvious symbolic details; for the esoteric symbols, such as those which may be discovered through the colours, or through the underlying graphic structures, find little disagreement between the Marseille pack and the Varallo. This is fortunate on a practical level, for the French set is readily available in both England and France, whilst the Varallo is commonly used in Italy.

Direct symbolism is at once obvious yet subtle in these two packs, for although the majority of them are clear on one level, the more they are meditated upon, the more their form allows a wide variety of interpretation. For example, the falling man in the House of God may be taken as a direct symbol of catastrophe, but when it is noted that he is isolated against the red brickwork of the tower, then the meaning of his fall becomes more apparent: again, the structure of his arms and legs add a further significance to his fall; and yet again his fall may be grasped on an altogether deeper level when the card is linked to the story preserved in the Golden Legend (fig. 176). Much of the direct symbolism may be fully understood only when it is considered in relation to its place in the sequence of the cards themselves. It has long been affirmed by commentators that each card has a meaning in relation to the traditional numerical sequence, and an additional meaning in regard to the inter relation of triadic affinities, but beyond this we find a rarification of meaning in certain of the isolated details within the cards. For example, if we examine the various items on the table before the Juggler in Arcanum 1, we see that what is intended is a double connotation, for on one level they represent the ordinary juggling paraphernalia, such as peas, dice and thimbles; at the same time they represent the embryonic form of the four symbols of the Minor Arcana. We see that the thimble is an embryonic Chalice; the knife, the Sword; the peas and dice, the Pentacle; and the rod, which the Juggler is holding in his left hand, is the Sceptre or Wand. The implication in this double connotation is obvious, then, for it suggests that the Juggler, who is everyman, has before him all the potential of these rich symbols – in other words, everyman has the possibility of spiritual vision and spiritual development – but he does not see their real potential or significance. These take on a new meaning when we link them with the zero Arcanum, the Fool, which deals with another aspect of man: the particular significance of these baubles, with all their spiritual promise, is emphasized by the presence of the sack on the table. This is evidently the sack which the Fool is carrying (see figures 24, 29) and we may presume from the symbolic reference that the things contained in the sack are the very baubles with which the Juggler is playing. The Juggler is at least examining the exoteric form of the baubles and cannot see their significance, cannot see through the *maya* of the world, but the Fool is merely weighed down by

THE JUGGLER

THE MAGICIAN.

THE MOON

THE SUN

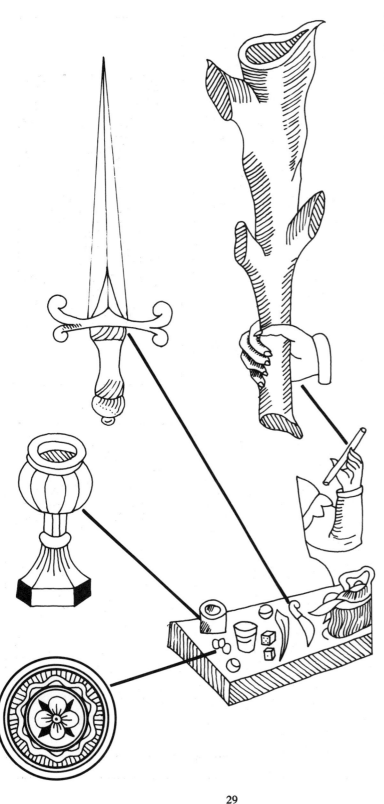

29

them – he does not even examine them, for they are locked away in the darkness of his bag, and he does not know why he carries the weight. The Fool card, within this symbolic structure, represents ordinary man caught up in the eternal round of material illusion: the Juggler card represents man who is both showing off, and yet interested in the questions raised by the baubles. It is significant that the Fool is moving, and that the Juggler is standing still! There are many 'interpenetrations' of meanings which link apparently isolated cards.

The symbolism of the Tarot on this level has been particularly damaged by 'restorers' of the Tarot, for the majority of new designs have lost the significance of the earlier packs through the sheer ignorance of the restorers, and in many cases symbols have been omitted or distorted because they were not correctly understood. For example, in the image of the Juggler which Papus reproduces, the baubles on the table have been transformed into the Pentacle, Sword, Chalice and Sceptre, thus losing the dual significance of the earlier Marseille card (figure 25). This same Arcanum was later transformed by Waite, who allowed the few sprouts of grass in the rocky foreground (evoking a mediaeval wasteland image) to grow luxuriantly under the pen of his illustrator into roses and lilies, 'to show the culture of aspiration', whatever that means! Certainly Waite succeeds in removing the arid desert upon which the Juggler stands, and therefore he succeeds in removing more than half the card's significance.

The colours of the cards have their own special symbolic meanings. Red denotes the active principle, the live-giving solar and martial energy, blue denotes the passive principle and its attendant devotion and receptivity of Venus; yellow denotes the spiritual quality, the life-force; and green denotes fertility, suggesting the idea of material forms which are invested with life. We shall occasionally note the significance of certain of the colours as we examine the cards individually, but the basic idea of the colours manifesting a meaningful relationship within the image itself is important to the correct understanding of the cards. We see confirmation of such colour symbolism in Arcanum 4, the Emperor, whose body and legs together form the glyph for Jupiter (see figure 76). The upper half of this card is the crescent of spiritual potential: it is red, and therefore active, which lends a strong spiritual quality to the card: the lower half represents the cross of matter, the radiating four elements which underlie the phenomenal world (figure 34) – this lower cross of materiality is blue, and therefore

29. The baubles on the table before the juggler are forms hiding their true significance.

30. The god Mercury, with his caduceus. This god is linked with both the first card in the set, 'The Juggler', and with the anima mundi of the last card, 'The World'.

31. 'The World'.

32. Anima Mercury as a female, from a seventeenth century alchemical text. The graphic association between these two images is very clear.

30   32

33

THE EMPEROR

34

35

passive. We find such symbolism in mediaeval Christian paintings – the golden halo of the Virgin suggests strong spiritual force, the blue of her mantle suggests passivity: she is being lifted up to heaven by the warm spirit of the halo. In the Emperor card, therefore, the graphic signs and the colours are in harmony, and the earthly and spiritual aspects of the Emperor are in their rightful place. The Devil, Arcanum 15, is wearing blue trousers, indicative of inertia, though the red belt about his loins suggests sexual force, and emphasizes the card's Scorpionic associations, for this sign rules the privy parts and the Scorpio colours are red and black. The image suggests that the evil which springs from the Devil is of a sexual kind, and is involved with the idea of sexual energies bursting out from a source which is in essence passive. In this card we see that he is standing on a red pedestal, which obviously suggests creativity as the basis for his activity: the reverse idea is suggested in those effigies which depict a knight standing on a writhing dragon. Again, the Juggler wears a hat which in its basic form is a lemniscate, traditionally representative of the re-conciliation of opposites (and therefore in vulgar imagery representative of eternity). The lemniscate has a series of deep meanings, but on one level it is an image of the meeting of sun and moon (figure 37). The colours of red and green are therefore of great significance considered in relation to the idea of the interaction of life (sun) on materiality (moon) pro-ducing life on earth: man is a compound lemniscate of solar and lunar forces. Each individual card must be examined along these lines for its full significance to be appreciated. Occasionally the force of the colour symbolism makes itself felt emotionally, though it is difficult to permit one's rational process to discover the meaning. The Moon, Arcanum 18, for example, is a powerful image of passive hell, largely with blue and yellow, but with a little red in the 'teardrop rays' suggesting that the baleful Moon takes its energy from the world below. This is an important idea in certain occult circles where it is maintained that the moon, in its role as the 'location' of hell, feeds on human suffering and misdeeds.

Each one of the individual *atout* images is built up from a basic graphic structure which throws much light on the significance of the cards. Sometimes we find details of graphic structure within the frame-work of the imagery; for instances, the arms of the Juggler are twisted in the shape of the Hebrew *Aleph* (figure 47); and the scythe of Death, Arcanum 13, interacts with the skeletal frame to echo the sign for Saturn (fig. 38), which was in mediaeval documents

33. The Sun and Moon meet in the strange shape of the slouch hat of the 'Juggler'.

34. 'The Emperor'.

35. Detail from 'Virgin and Child with Angels' by Fra Angelico (N.G., London). The traditional colours of Christian art are used in the Tarot cards, as are certain simple graphic devices.

36. 'The Devil' based on an eighteenth century card. Observe the parody of 'angelic attendants' (figure 35) in the two chained slaves.

37. 'The Devil' designed by Waite. Observe how the slaves have become male and female, thus losing much of the significance of the card.

THE DEVIL

36

THE DEVIL .

37

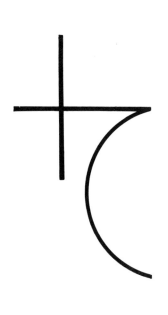

13

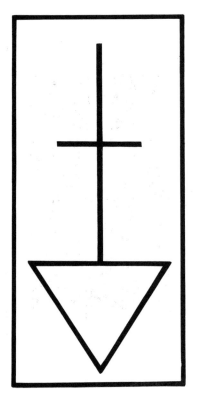

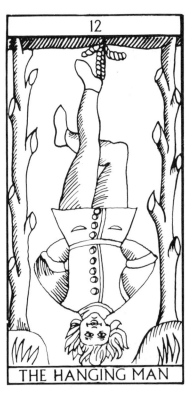

12

THE HANGING MAN

drawn as an inverted Jupiter, thus indicating limitations, fears and death. Sometimes, however, we find that the entire card is arranged in such a way as to be interpreted in terms of graphics. One example is found in the image of the Hanging Man, Arcanum 12. The head and arms, which are tied behind his back, form an inverted triangle, and his legs form a cross: the whole graphic image is one of the cross of materiality weighing down an inverted triangle, the meaning of which we shall touch upon at page 67. This curious abstract graphic is tied into the square formed by the gibbet and the earth, a square which is the symbol for the containing materiality of the four elements.

The most commonly recurring graphic forms are the triangle, square, diagonal and cross, the main significances of which will be dealt with at the appropriate parts of the following analyses. In simple terms, the triangle indicates spiritual balance and harmony when it is resting on its base, for it is a symbol of the trinity, the three *gunas*, the astrological quadruplicities, and so on (figure 42). The square is a symbol of materiality in that it represents the area enclosed by the four elements of Earth, Air, Fire and Water, which are the 'matter' of life (figure 42). A diagonal which cuts a square into two triangles (figure 42) suggests the idea of passive materiality being vivified by triadic action, which is always spiritual. The cross is formed from the meeting of two apices (as revealed in our study of the Wheel of Fortune, page 62), in which case it is considered a dynamic spiritual force; or it is formed from two lines crossing, in which case it is considered to be the meeting of two unlike or even contradictory forces, as exemplified in the analysis of the Hanging Man at page 70.

The force of the cross and the square may be regarded as being very similar, but they do in fact connote different philosophies. Like the cross, the square is a symbol of materiality, though it differs in enclosing an area: this enclosed area represents the mysterious fifth element, called by Pythagoras the *Akashya*, which is the invisible life force permeating all matter. Thus, the area enclosed by the four elements of the square is just as important as the square itself (figure 39). In ordinary exoteric interpretation the square represents passivity, the 'human condition', or 'the weight or cross to be carried', which is essentially a statement of the spirit (descending/ascending plane) meeting the resistance of material inertia (horizontal plane). On a deeper level of interpretation, however, the invisible *Akashya* is taken into account, and what is important in the square is not merely the limitations of the four elemental walls, the 'bounds and bonds of the world', but the invisible world of spirit contained within the four elements. It is almost a parable of the degeneration of man that we should think that the ancients taught of the existence of four elements when they in fact taught of five, the last being the unifying, although invisible, life force which permeates all materiality. In the mechanical model of the universe we have today, there is no place for the invisible *Akashya* – and yet the ancients put this first, indicating that the other four merely serve this one. We see this esoteric significance in the Hanging Man, where the symbolism proclaims that what is important is the invisible condition of man, for he is pictured as hanging upside-down within the space of the *Akashya*. Because this life force is invisible, man does not see his condition, does not realize that he is hanging upside-down, which explains why he is smiling!

Further details of the deep symbolism of these cards will gradually be revealed with practice, along the lines suggested at page 129. It will be found that one cannot really understand the cards in any deep sense until one uses them in actual practice, within formal patterns in response to questions. Only with such practice may the full living force of the cards be experienced. For this reason the beginner is advised to read the following text carefully, and then immediately attempt to put what has been learned into practice, through attempting serious readings. After a short period of practice one may then return to a study of the text, which will considerably re-vitalize and enrich the understanding of the cards. Those who wish to gain any further insight into the Major Arcana must try to discover analogies and relationships for themselves. The following section deals with each of the Major cards in some detail, but the interpretation is by no means exhaustive. It must be understood that the whole point of hieroglyphics is that their content is always a little more than may be adequately explained in words: this is the major difficulty which confronts any teacher of the Tarot.

SPIRIT

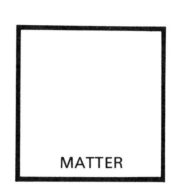

MATTER

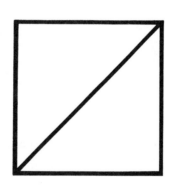

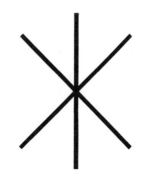

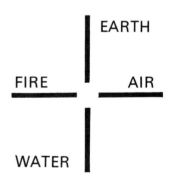

EARTH

FIRE   AIR

WATER

38. The symbol for Saturn, linked with death. The half crescent, which represents potential spirit, is echoed in the curved back and leg of the skeleton.

39. The graphic analysis of 'The Hanging Man'.

40. The thirteenth card, though usually printed without a name, is called 'The Death'.

41. 'The Hanging Man' is neither tied to his gibbet, nor unhappy at his situation. He is everyman.

42. The basic structures underlying the graphic designs of the Tarot cards. The triangle on its base represents spiritual values: on its apex, spiritual values in chaos. The square symbolises matter, whilst the four lines of the cross link with the four elements underlying matter. The six-pointed star is explained at figure 128.

42

43. 'The Magician' designed
by the occultist Crowley, as
the first of the Major Arcana.
The symbols incorporated in
this card are from many
different sources, mainly
Egyptian, and the composite
nature of the card makes it too
esoteric for general use.

44. 'The Juggler', based on an
eighteenth century original.

45. 'The Juggler' designed by
Wirth (see bibliography) for
his own Tarot pack.

43

24

The following series of short essays on each of the Major cards is designed to help the beginner to gather in his own mind a number of relevant associations which will enable him to touch some of the deeper levels of meaning when examining them within a formal pattern in response to a question. Mainly out of historical interest I list certain of the traditional 'fixed meanings' of the cards, even in those cases where I myself do not agree with these. I give also the interpretation for a card when it is 'reversed' (that is, when it appears in a formal pattern upside-down, due to shuffling), though I do not think that a reversed card necessarily implies a reversed meaning, and even though my own method of interpretation requires that the cards are shuffled so that they never appear reversed (see page 129). The first card of the Major Arcana, The Juggler, is meant to represent man as he is. It is an image of a mountebank or juggler standing at a table upon which are spread all the paraphernalia of his trade: thimbles, dice, cups, coins and a knife out of its sheath. In his left hand he holds a rod, and in his right hand a coin which (some say) he is about to make disappear (figure 44).

This image is an incredibly rich statement of man's state of being in his normal level of consciousness. It presents mankind as a strangely garbed individual acting to an invisible audience. By a clever stratagem, the audience is, of course, whoever is looking at the card, being amused or intrigued by what he sees there, and he becomes this everyman Juggler by identifying with him. The card is essentially a commentary on man as an actor of different roles, with little or no identity of his own: 'distracted from distraction by distraction.' The worthless objects on the table before him, with which he is entertaining his audience, or merely passing away his own time, are actually the primitive forms of the four great symbols of the Minor pack. The coins and dice represent the crude and esoteric form of the Pentacle (figure 29); the knife represents the Sword (figure 29); the cup or thimble represents the Chalice (figure 29), and the rod which he holds in his left hand represents the Sceptre (figure 29). The implications are that the Juggler is unaware of the great potential of these things, which he is using merely for his own distraction or to entertain others – just as the average man is unaware of the mystery of life which surrounds him, and which he takes so much for granted. Instead of making some use of the potential greatness of his baubles, instead of attempting to develop what he has before him, he is content to play with them and to use them merely to

Card 1   The Juggler

THE JUGGLER

44

1 LE BATELEVR

45

46. Derivation of the lemniscate hat of 'The Juggler'.

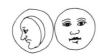

47. The Hebrew Aleph *anthropomorphized, to show a connection with the strange gesture of the Juggler, and the link with the first letter of the alphabet.*

48. A schema showing how the
49. tripartite division of the card is derived from the glyph for Mercury.

50. Mercury, with his glyph above his head, and his snake-entwined staffs in his hands.

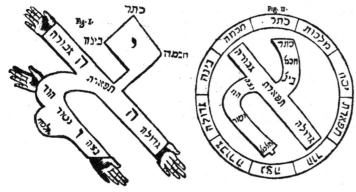

302 OEDIPI ÆGYPTIACI GYMNAS. HIEROGL.

De quibus ita Pardes in porta שער עמיח id eſt, ſciorum.

והנה רצוננו לכתוב צורת האדם העליון בצורת אלף
לרמוז כי כולו יחוד שלם אע"פ שנאת עשר שמות
דברים מחולקים כולו יחוד וזה הורה בדמות אלף ויש קצת
סמך לדעת זה כדברי הרשב"י ע"ה בספר התיקונים כי
כוונת צורת השם שהוא עשר ספירות כנודע בצורת אלף
לרמוז אל עשר מיוחדים אחדות שוה אחדות שלימה בשם
בן ארבע אותיות:

Et ecce intentio eſt nobis deſcribere figuram hominis ſupremi ſub figura א *Alphal*

distract himself. It is interesting that the hand holding the coin points towards the earth, while the Host (the perfect expression of the Pentacle, of which the coin is the base form) finds its highest fulfilment held aloft. Later annotators of the Tarot appear to have missed the deep significance of these 'baubles' and invariably changed them into the four symbols of the suits (as in figure 29), thus reducing the whole force of this card. The meaning is quite clear – the Juggler is not aware of the potential of the baubles which he has taken out of his sack: any card which depicts them as symbols of the suit is reversing the meaning implicit in the card. The circle is both a symbol of eternity (figure 49), and a symbol of the spiritual world – in this card it is being held downwards. The straight line, or the cross, imaged in the rod held by our everyman, is a symbol of the material world – but in this picture it is being held up, in the place proper to spiritual forces. In these two basic symbols, we have an intimation that everyman is reversing the natural order of things, to judge from the look on his distracted face, *because he does not know any better!*

The card as a whole is cut into two main areas by the top of the table. The upper half contains the head and torso of the man, and the lower half contains his legs and feet, the table and the earth. These two divisions correspond to the division between heaven and earth. The top half represents the heavenly nature of man. In this upper half we see the strange gesture which the Juggler is making, with one hand pointing up to the sky and one pointing down to the earth, the whole posture echoing the form of the first Hebrew letter *Aleph* (figure 48). The gesture therefore affirms the initiatory force of this first card, and implies that the heavenly side of man is required by its own nature to move in a spiritual direction. There is an impression of choice in the way the man is balancing the rod and the coin in his two hands, and one feels that he is perhaps awakening to a perception of the baubles' great potential. The cabbalistic ideogram at figure 47 is based on *Aleph*, and indicates the strong resemblance between the gesture made by the Juggler, and the basic Hebrew letter.

The curious broad-brimmed hat, which resembles a pilgrim's slouch hat, is actually in the form of a lemniscate, a sideways figure eight, which is often regarded as the symbol for eternity. This ancient symbol is probably derived from the idea of the sun and moon being linked together (as in figure 46), and besides concentrating the image within the celestial sphere, it indicates the idea of reconciling

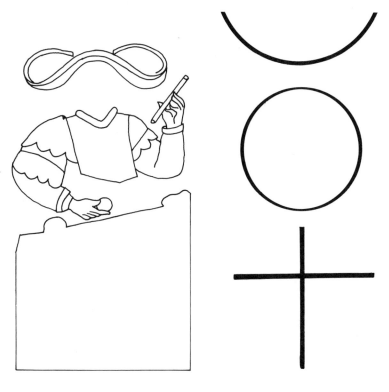

opposites, of yoking together the female (moon) and male (sun) principles – an idea which crops up again and again in the Tarot pack. The attempt to reconcile the sun and the moon – that is, in psychological terms, the attempt to bring into harmony the conscious and subconscious – is the purpose behind magic and alchemy, and therefore the concern of the Tarot. The symbol of this attained purpose (the lemniscate) is the interlinked sun and moon, which is taken as a symbol of eternity, of eternal life, a life not subject to the mutability of the planetary movements. Our everyman stands between heaven and earth, and contains within him a cacophony of forces all searching in different directions (his garb is multi-coloured, but the predominating colour is red, suggesting that he is less passive in the celestial sphere than in the terrestrial). Above him is the promise of eternal life, below him, the baubles which take his attention.

The first card is one of the 'astrological series', and is associated with Gemini. We may see this association from the fact that the card's structure recalls both the Caduceus (figure 50) and the glyph for Mercury (figure 49), which is the ruler of Gemini. Like the triadic glyph of Mercury, the card itself is divided into three main areas – there is the division created by the table top, which makes of the lower part of the card a kind of lopsided square, in which the feet of the table and the feet of the man are firmly planted on the ground.

The second division is the central one, occupied by the arms held in that strange gesture which resembles half a reversed fylfot (figure 48), but which in fact consists of one arm pointing down to the earth, and one pointing up to the skies. It is no accident that the hand which points down towards the earth holds a circle (be it a coin or a magical disk), and the hand which points up to the heavens holds a stick, for of course the circle is a symbol of heaven, and the stick is part of the cross and therefore a symbol of materiality (figure 42). The idea conveyed here is that the heavenly forces contain within them a quality of the earth, whilst the material qualities contain always an element of heaven, so that nothing is entirely separated from anything else. In this context the circular fylfot motion of forces, each with the seeds of the opposite contained within them, recall the circular *yin* and *yang* symbol (figure 52), the black *yin* containing a spot of white *yang*, and the *yang* containing a spot of black *yin*. The white *yang* spot is the equivalent of the circle held in the lower hand of the Juggler. The dark *yin* spot is the equivalent of the rod (materiality)

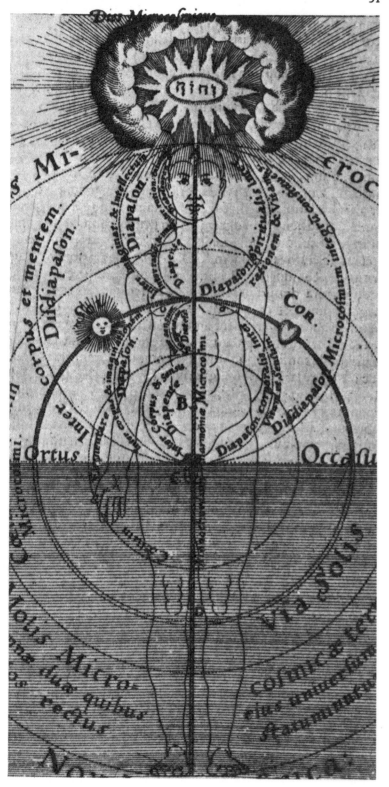

held in the upper hand of the Juggler. It is of considerable importance that the arms of the man should be utilized to express this idea, for Gemini itself rules the arms, and that the fylfot movement should suggest the wheel of eternal motion, which is also a Geminian concern.

The third division of the card is found in the head, which superficially may be taken as being surmounted by an *upside-down* crescent, completely at variance with the spirit-bearing crescent of the Mercury glyph. In fact, as we have seen, this large hat, placed on the head, the seat of the intellect (which is the domain of Mercury, as of Gemini), is in the form of a figure eight, expressive of eternity. This hat appears once more in the Tarot pack in the eleventh card, Strength, but this time on the head of a woman, the *atout* which is associated with Aries (figure 137).

This three-way division of the card therefore corresponds to the triadic unity of the symbol for Mercury (figure 50). The glyph for Mercury is itself tripartite – a cross, a circle and a semi-circle (figure 49) – obviously linking with the earth, the sun and the moon (see figure 73). This remarkable picture is an uncompromising image of everyman juggling with his own destiny, concerned with self and with an unreal audience, and apparently unaware of the drama of heavenly and telluric forces around him. The lower half of the *atout* contains the table, the Juggler's baubles, the earth, and the legs of the table, and between them these represent the conditions of earth. The earth itself is almost barren, though the odd sprouts of grass suggest that there is potential growth even here, just as there is potential in the baubles. The square top of the table confirms the idea of earth (see page 25), and the three visible legs of the table (where *is* the fourth? – by all the laws of perspective the fourth should be visible) suggest the 'law of three' being grounded in the material world, the creative triad which permeates all life. The image as a whole is the visual equivalent of the Paracelsian idea of man as the midpoint between heaven and earth: he is a product of earth, and his feet are firmly planted on the earth, but he is also a product of heaven, and his head is thrust into the heavenly symbol of eternity – but, of course, the Juggler is unaware of his greatness, of his origin or his destiny. He is calmly amusing himself or others with silly little tricks and illusions, while the sun moves overhead and the earth moves below; he is unaware of what he might become if only he would see the world aright instead of concentrating on his histrionic juggling with baubles. Man is a tension between heaven and earth, oblivious of the great forces which gave him life, perpetuate his existence, and which will surely bring him death. This is the potential of life – and, indeed, one senses that the Juggler appears to be hesitating in his gesture of benediction, as though he is subconsciously prepared for the spiritual adventure promised by the sequence of cards.

When the Juggler appears in a formal pattern it usually indicates that a change is required, especially a change in attitude. Any of the associations raised in the previous analysis may be taken as relevant to the particular question which gave rise to the formal pattern. The fragmentation of colours in this card suggests a need for the querent to 'pull things together', to organize either himself or his situation, and to assess his position in a new way. Why does the Juggler feel compelled to act to an audience, and who is the audience? This is the question which all people must ask in the face of problems linked with relationships. In a reading for a female querent this card may sometimes suggest a male who is not entirely satisfactory for the querent: one who is somehow lacking in 'quality of being', is ultimately unreliable, or is somehow unable to accept responsibilities.

The traditional divinatory interpretation of the card is that the Juggler indicates 'the commencement of activity' and the mercurial impulse towards speech, acting or the written world. It indicates the ability to take risks, as well as alert intelligence and persuasive eloquence. In reverse it indicates charlatanism, cowardice and deceit. On a deep level, any of the philosophical implications involved with the reconciling of opposites, the development of self as a spiritual exercise within the framework of ordinary life, and man's blindness to his own spiritual condition, may be linked with this card when it is dealt for a reading. A study of the dual zodiacal sign Gemini is essential for a correct understanding of this card.

The Juggler is sometimes called the Minstrel, Wizard, Magus, Mountebank, Gypsy Master and (rarely) the Pagat. The latter word Pagat is supposed to be derived from Bagat or Paghead and Gad, signifying fortune; whilst the card is sometimes called *Bagatto*, as the objects on the table have been confused with cobbling tools.

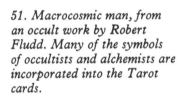

51. Macrocosmic man, from an occult work by Robert Fludd. Many of the symbols of occultists and alchemists are incorporated into the Tarot cards.

52. The yin yang *sigmoid circle, surrounded by the eight trigrams of the Chinese I Ching.*

53. Early lemniscates. Top, third millenium B.C. Bottom, mediaeval.

54. 'The Lady Pope', based on eighteenth century designs.

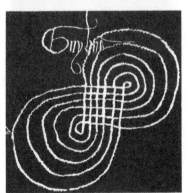

THE LADY POPE

55. *Title page of a book on the legendary Pope Joan, linked with the second card of the Major pack.*

56. *Frontpiece from 'Pope Joan', showing the Lady Pope giving birth.*

57. *'The Lady Pope'. The cross in the inner lozenge is significant of spiritual birth, since the area relates to the womb – see also figure 35.*

58. *Graphic analysis of 'The Lady Pope' to show the trinity resting securely on the cross of materiality.*

A Present for a Papist:
OR THE
LIFE and DEATH
OF
POPE JOAN,
Plainly Proving
Out of the Printed Copies, and
Manuscripts of Popish Writers and
others, that a Woman called
JOAN, was really
POPE of ROME;
And was there Deliver'd of a Bastard
Son in the open Street, as She went
in Solemn Procession.

By a LOVER of TRUTH;
Denying Human Infallibility.

LONDON,
Printed for T. D. and are to be sold at
the Ship in St. Mary Axe, and by
most Booksellers, 1675.

55

A Woman Pope (as History doth tell)
In High Procession Shee in Labour fell,
And was Deliver'd of a Bastard Son ;
Thenc Rome some call The Whore of Babylon.

56

The second card is meant to represent the passive side of human beings. It is generally interpreted as being an image of a Lady Pope, presumably the legendary Pope Joan (figure 56), with an open book on her knees (figure 57). The first card is male, and in an active posture; this second card is female, and in a passive, contemplative posture.

The image is a careful statement of the passive conditions necessary to the development of the spiritual possibilities represented by the first Arcanum. Blue is the predominating colour, traditionally the colour of sensitive passivity. The opening of the blue cape, with red inside, suggests a vaginal shape, emphasizing the receptive quality of passivity and hence sensitivity: the idea of creative generation enfolded within a cloak of passive blue. The basic shapes of the image also emphasize this idea, for the lower part of the card is in fact a square, cut off by the horizontal line created by the fold of the cloak, the sleeve, the hand and the book. This is the square of materiality. On top of this is balanced a triangle, its base on top of the square, on the line formed by the arm and book, its apex being the crown which the 'Popess' is wearing. Since the vertical axis of this triangle is greater than the base, the triangle has an upward movement, and therefore the meaning of the triangular form is evolutory (figure 58). The whole symbol is of an evolutory triadic force; perhaps the 'three' legs of the table, rooted in the materiality of the previous card, are now seen on a higher level, resting firmly on the passive materiality of the square, instead of being contained in the square. This is the force of the imagery of those Gothic sculpted portals, with the columns on either side of the square decorated with scenes from this life, and the triangular area above the entrance covered with scenes of heavenly life. The connotation is one of great inner striving, of balance and fitness of position. The triangle resting on the material square suggests the world in a state of order, in comparison with the disorder prevalent in this previous card: the triangle is firmly balanced, and in ascendency over the emblem of materiality.

Behind the head of the Lady Pope is a double wimple. We shall study the evolution of these wimples as we examine the sequence of cards. The Popess has been identified by various commentators with the horned Isis, and it is very probable that the wimples are meant to suggest horns, which represent strength (because they are penetrating) and receptivity (because their outline is like a receptacle). Later editions of the Tarot placed two

THE LADY POPE

57

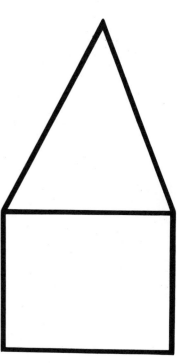

58

31

THE EMPRESS

THE EMPEROR

THE POPE

THE LOVERS

columns behind the Popess, and sometimes even transformed the wimples into a veil between the columns. One column was supposed to denote activity and the other passivity. These changes served only to distort the true meaning of the card, for the wimples do change into columns with such significance later on in the Arcana (see figures 57, 60 and 102), and there is nothing to be gained by spoiling the crescent form of the wimple and placing such columns behind the figure. In its sequence, following on the Juggler, it is clear that the receptive 'horns' or wimple are a graphic comment on the nature of the passivity required for the development of those latent spiritual potentials we saw in the Juggler. The slouch hat of the Juggler is enclosed, signifying the perpetual struggle between female moon and male sun, while the 'horns' of the Popess are open and receptive, implying that receptivity and quiescence are necessary for the development of the human spirit. The crescent shape has long been regarded both as a symbol of feminine passivity and as a symbol of paradise, and is most obviously so in the ancient astrological symbol for the moon (figure 73). Clearly, the idea is that man must still himself, and open to experiences in the realm of the spirit (the wimples, like the slouch hat, are cut by the top of the card, suggesting contact with the celestial sphere), if he is to make the right choice between heaven and earth, and if he is to develop inwardly. The book on the knees of the Popess reiterates this idea; an obvious symbol of knowledge, the book is also open, thus suggesting that contemplation of ideas and the search for knowledge will lead in the right direction. Taken in sequence, with the Lady Pope on the right of the Juggler, we see that the Lady Pope is offering the book to the Juggler but he is looking away, apparently engrossed in his display. The book is obviously a dual symbol, relating to the phenomena of life as well as to knowledge and learning which at best can only reflect such phenomena. This perhaps explains the curious tilting of the Juggler's face, for even as he plays with the baubles, he does not look at them: he is looking to his right. The posture he holds is too awkward to be accidental, so we must take it that he is looking away from the following card, The Lady Pope, the symbol of religion and light. In other words, the first card represents man in the midst of a wonder – the meeting of spiritual and material forces – who finds a level of awareness sufficient only to occupy himself with cheap material things, with display, and to turn his face away from the source of his spiritual being.

An interesting graphic idea is expressed in the shape formed by the edges of the cape, the top of the book, and left arm of the figure. This red lozenge (figure 54) within the blue cape (and thus the entry into the vagina, into the womb), is material and active, for its four-sided, inner, knowledge (red colour and the book) will help the development of the everyman of the first *atout*.

In a formal pattern, this card suggests any of the philosophical implications involved with the development of the contemplative life within the framework of intellectual and spiritual withdrawal, as well as man's sensitivity to his own real spiritual needs. Very often this 'spiritual' side is given a real material expression in a reading for a male querent, as it frequently symbolizes a woman with whom he is interested in establishing a relationship, or with whom a relationship is ending: the keynote is disengagement, for it does not relate to a woman with whom he is contemporaneously linked. In a certain sense, the card relates to the 'ideal' or to the 'dream woman', and on this level it is clearly linked with the *anima*, the female soul-mate, for the entire card emphasizes this lunar, feminine side of human duality. The moon of the lemniscate above the head of the Juggler is thus partly explored by this card.

The traditional divinatory interpretation of the card is that the Popess indicates intuition, hidden things, and the influence of the moon and Saturn, though the latter tradition is extremely dubious. It indicates silence, the need for silence, a stranger, and 'religious feeling'. In reverse the card is supposed to indicate laziness, bigotry, excessive imagination, and hostile intentions – in traditional astrological terms, the lunar forces under pressure or weakly placed.

The Lady Pope is sometimes called Pope Joan, the Archpriestess, Female Pontiff, Wise Woman and Gipsy Witch. In certain systems the card is held to represent the goddess Isis (figure 67), and it has been suggested by Van Rensselaer that the name Papessa is merely a corruption of the word Isis: on these grounds he repudiates all contact with Pope Joan. The Hebrew letter *Beth* on the Italian pack (figure 65) contains the idea of 'mouth or tongue' and may be linked with the expression of the law. Since she stands as the first of the female cards in the major cards, she is often claimed to represent the inquirer.

Johannæ Papisfæ

59. 'The Empress'.

60. 'The Pope'. ·

61. 'The Emperor'.

62. 'The Lovers'. These last four cards are based on eighteenth century originals.

63. Pope Joan, with her child. Observe the similarity between the crown she wears, and that worn by 'The Lady Pope'.

64. An Italian version of 'The Juggler' card.

65. An Italian version of 'The Lady Pope'.

IL BAGATTEL.

LA PAPESSA

66. An Italian version of 'The Empress'.

67. The goddess Isis, who has been linked with several of the cards, including 'The Empress'.

68. 'The Empress'.

69. Graphic analysis of 'The Empress'. The womb-like lozenge, containing the cross, which we saw in the previous card, is expanded here to fill the whole human form.

66

67

The third card is meant to represent the force resulting from the meeting between the Juggler and the Lady Pope. The image is that of an Empress, seated, bearing in her left hand a sceptre, and in her right hand a heraldic shield.

This image represents the evolutory outcome of the course adopted by the Juggler in his decision to put aside his baubles and to look for the real meaning in life. We see that the wimple has evolved into wings, which connote a heavenly relationship, and perhaps an emphasis on the solar nature of the two elements (lunar and solar) contained within the hat of the Juggler, suggesting the idea of spiritual achievements being the outcome of his chosen course. The basic shape emphasizes the inner quality of this card, for the droop of clothing between the knees, and the head with its double crown, are the bottom and top points of a lozenge-shaped quaternity (figure 69). The implication is that the same small lozenge which we saw in the previous card (figure 57) has now grown, the potential has been developed, and the whole image is one of fecundity and inner life. The sceptre, which is surely a link with the Sceptre of the Minor Arcana, remind us of the baton which the Juggler held, also in the left hand; the implication is that the potential of the baton, or magic wand, has also been realized, and its value is now clearly recognized. The symbol on top of the sceptre has ben related to the astrological sign for Venus ($\venus$), but it is in fact more precisely the cross ($\pm$) described by Cirlot as the 'higher ternary acting upon the spiritual quaternary' – which is a precise summary of the nature of this card.

The Juggler held a coin in his right hand, the Lady Pope held the book, and now the Empress holds a shield emblazoned with an eagle. The connexion can be seen when we understand the spiritual idea associated with the eagle; it was believed to be capable of flying higher than any other bird and, presumably for this reason, has from ancient times been taken as a symbol of the ability to dominate the baser qualities of life, and to rise spiritually: it was at one time associated with the zodiacal sign Scorpio, and is itself ruled by the expansive planet Jupiter. In alchemy the eagle symbolized volatilization. We trace the elementary coin held by the Juggler, transmuted through knowledge and learning to the Host, represented in an allegorical form as the symbol of spiritual ascendancy. The relationship between the eagle and the Empress herself offers the possibility of an interesting line of thought, for they both have wings,

Card 3   The Empress

THE EMPRESS

68

THE EMPRESS

69

70. *An Italian version of 'The Devil'. Observe the bat-like wings.*

71. *Solar wings, more like the wings of a bird than those associated with the devil.*

72. *The Solar wings associated with the angels contrasted with the leathery wings of a demon (from Ghiberti's Baptistry doors, Florence). The wings of 'The Empress' forms a crescent, in much the same way as the wings of 'The Devil', but what the crescent will contain is determined by the nature of the wings themselves.*

XV

IL DIAVOLO

prononce ta demande

and the fold of clothing around the knees of the Empress certainly echoes the curved lower part of the heraldic shield: thus, in a graphic sense, the Empress is the eagle as well as being the spiritual version of the Juggler, and we may take it that the Juggler everyman has learned to fly, or at least now has the potential of flight.

It is not known why the Empress should precede the Emperor in the pack, though it has naturally been suggested (without much tangible evidence) that this is a relic of matriarchal rule. In terms of the triadic order, however, the curious position of the Empress must be expected, for the Emperor in third place would in fact break the sequence of development. It is essential that the Juggler, in his search for inner meaning, and in his alchemical urge to transmute the baubles before him into symbols of a different order, should become more receptive and sensitive; in a word, become more feminine! The presence of this card in a formal pattern suggests a strong spiritual force – a spiritual ease which is feminine, even though linked with solar and Jupiterian forces. In a reading for a man it may represent the object of the subject's love.

The traditional divinatory interpretation of the card is that the Empress indicates wisdom, spiritual strength, the evolutory trends of civilization, and the influence of the moon and sun. The card is sometimes linked more with Venus in its obvious connotation of femininity and fecundity, but we may see the reason for the former planetary associations contained in the Juggler's hat, for the card represents the development of the spiritual state of awareness which is open to the bemused Juggler. The Empress is therefore, on a deeper level of meaning, emblematic of the soul of everyman. It indicates comprehension, elegance, feminine domination, intelligence and splendour. In reverse it indicates coquetry, vanity, a lack of practicality, frivolity and prodigality.

The Hebrew letter *Gimel* on the Italian card (figure 66) is linked with the idea of enclosure, which finds a correspondence in the graphic structure of the card (figure 69): the letter is also associated with the throat and speech. The 'angelic' nature of the wings (see figures 71 and 72) indicates that the speech will be friendly, helpful and constructive speech, unlike that of the Devil card, for whom the Hebrew *Zain* (figure 70) is associated with destruction.

The Empress is sometimes called Isis, Eve, Lilith, and Gypsy Queen.

72

73. *The crescent of the Moon, the solar disc and the cross of earth, forming the glyph for Mercury.*

74. *The three-headed 'Mercury' of the alchemists. The wings link with the devil, whilst the serpentine coils of the tail may be associated with Scorpio, which has rule over snakes.*

75. *'The Emperor'.*

76. *Analysis of 'The Emperor' to show the crescent pulling up the cross of matter, as in the glyph for Jupiter.*

73

74

The fourth card, the Emperor, represents man as he might be, and it is the male counterpart of the Empress. The card therefore expresses the active attributes of those qualities examined in the previous card: in other words, they are the masculine and positive expression of the potentials hinted at in the Juggler.

The image is meant to represent the outcome of the initial ascendancy of the spirit over the physical and baser elements. We see that the body and head of the Emperor form a crescent shape which may be followed through from the lower curve of the curious helmet, down the bend of the entire arm which rests on the curved armrest of the chair, and continues along the lower part of his short tunic (figure 76). Beneath this large crescent the legs are crossed, and the strangely uncomfortable posture of the Emperor is thus meant to represent the symbol for Jupiter, which is that of a crescent surmounting a cross (figure 76). Jupiter is the planet of expansion, and governs beneficent authority. It is interesting to relate this to the symbol for the restrictive planet Saturn, which is the cross weighing down the half-circle (figure 38). The force of the Jupiter symbol is meant to convey the idea of spiritual ascendancy over the cross of materiality. The crescent is half of the circle, which is in itself a symbol for the sun (see figures 73 and 74), and thus besides receptivity it suggests the idea of a force requiring completion – it is an *anima* requiring an *animus*. The Platonic tradition teaches that no spirit is complete in itself whilst on earth, and before it may achieve completion must find a corresponding soul with which to unite. Thus the *animus*, or male principle, must find its *anima*, or female principle, in the form of another person, in order to achieve inner harmony. The meeting of two souls is the act of 'falling in love'. In astrology and alchemy the moon is the *anima*, and the sun is the *animus*. Seen in this context, the lemniscate symbol (figure 46) takes on a deeper significance, for besides being a graphic device showing the union of opposites, and besides symbolizing a 'timeless' state (eternity), it is also a perfect symbol of love – the meeting of the lunar *anima* with the solar *animus*. This fourth card shows the completion of the female passivity which was required of the Juggler if he were to evolve in a spiritual direction.

The graphic development of the cards expressive of this spiritual direction is shown in figure 81. In each case we find a symbol for materiality in the lower half of the card, and in the top half we see different states of spiritual development, or poten-

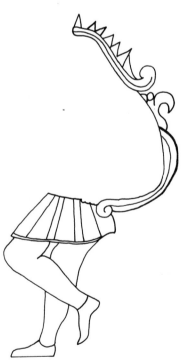

75   76

39

1

SPIRIT

LUNAR–
SOLAR

LUNAR
TRINITY

2

SPIRIT

MATTER

TRIADIC
EARTH

FECUND
EARTH

MATTER

THE JUGGLER

THE LADY POPE

3

SPIRIT

WINGED
SPIRIT
IN TRINITY

POTENTIAL
SPIRIT
IN TRINITY

4

SPIRIT

MATTER

EAGLE
LIFTED
ABOVE
FECUND
EARTH

GROUNDED
EAGLE
NEXT TO
MATERIAL
CROSS

MATTER

THE EMPRESS

THE EMPEROR

tial. In the Emperor, which marks the point of transition as well as the final outcome of the triadic action, the spiritual development and potential is most simply stated; it is in ascendancy over the material qualities expressed in the Juggler, and the 'situation' suggested by the relationship of the two simple graphic forms is one ripe for inner or spiritual development. As in the image of the Empress we find a heraldic eagle on a small shield, and a sceptre. This time, however, the sceptre is held in the right hand, and its position in relation to the crescent form has a phallic connotation, suggesting that the following sequence of cards will deal with the development of fertilization of the spirit. In certain popular teachings, as indeed in occultism, the right hand suggests activity, the left passivity, and so once more the underlying theme of the card is hinted at by the device. The red (always symbolic of activity) of his cloak seems to support this idea of the initiation of a new active and creative phase.

It is difficult to explain the position of the heraldic eagle in this *atout*. The best explanation which occurs to me is that since the sequence of cards in the following triad deals with the questions of decisions and right conduct involved with spiritual development, the eagle is 'grounded' – it has been placed on the ground next to the cross of materiality in order to indicate that spiritual flights are not required at this stage of development. One must concentrate on the conditions around one, with the conditions which life itself offers, if one is to develop inwardly. The fact that the wings of the Emperor's eagle point downwards, whilst those in the third Arcanum point upwards, supports this theory.

In a formal pattern the card indicates strong authority, or perhaps a need to consult it. One may think of the image for the expansive Jupiter, and relate this directly to the place the card holds in the pattern: the direction in which he looks is important in relation in the question asked, for this indicates which way the Jupiterian urge is being directed.

The traditional divinatory interpretation of the card is that the Emperor indicates the will, executive strength, material wealth and the influence of Saturn and Mars, in spite of the obvious Jupiterian force. It indicates the power of public authority, law, perseverance, resolute strength and certainty. In reverse it indicates dogmatism, a weak character, fear of authority and grave misrepresentation.

The Emperor is sometimes called Osiris, the Gypsy King, and the Guardian of the Holy Grail.

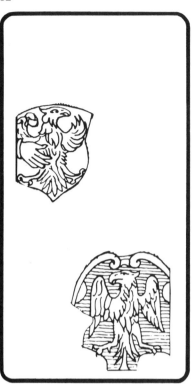

77. 'The Juggler'.

78. 'The Empress'.

79. The upper part (Spiritual) of the first four cards present different aspects of Spirituality, whilst the lower halves deal with matter in its four-fold element of state.

80. 'The Lady Pope'.

81. 'The Emperor'.

82. The shields from 'The Empress' and 'The Emperor', the former with wings in flight, half way up the card, the latter with wings at rest, at the bottom of the card.

83. A fifteenth century mnemonic figure. The angels at the top, and the devil at the bottom, emphasise the sense of spirituality in the topmost part of the pictorial area, as seen in figure 82 above.

83

Von dem vnnützen koften der gelegt würt von dem ge=
meinen folck, vff meß lefen, fübenden, dreifigften vnd iar=
tagen ıc.

84. *An Italian version of 'The Pope'.*

85. *A priest introducing a fool to a devil. The priest stands as 'mediator' between two forces, as do many central figures and symbols in the Tarot pack. Triadic action lies at the very foundations of occultism.*

86. *'The Pope'.*

87. *The graphic analysis of 'The Pope'. The two circles will grow into solar and lunar discs, below the trinity.*

84

85

The fifth card is meant to express certain ideas linked with instruction. It is an image of a Pope blessing two cardinals who kneel before him. One cardinal is pointing downwards, the other upwards, and this evokes the gesture of the Juggler in the first Arcanum. Clearly these two cardinals are the active and passive forms of the Juggler, the personifications of the moon and sun of the slouch hat, come to earth and in need of instruction. The Pope himself, who is instructing them (blessing them with a gesture), is the masculine side of the qualities we examined in the Popess – here knowledge is not acquired passively, but propagated actively. The wimple of the Lady Pope is now more obviously of a phallic import, for it is presented as two columns framing the triple crown; these no longer suggest the passivity of the crescent shape, but are clearly active in form, though complementary in colour. The triple cross has been explained as a *lingam*, suggesting the generative power of the world, and we see that this cross actually forms one end of the crescent created by the left arm of the Pope and the fold of drapery which runs right through to the head of the cardinal on the left of the card. Obviously, the idea is that the fertilization hinted at in the fourth Arcanum has now been accomplished, for the receptive crescent and the phallic sign are now one (figure 86). This crescent rests on the lower square enclosing the cardinals who are, it will be noted, quite separate from one another.

The enclosing of two human beings in a square of materiality echoes very clearly the ideas of *anima* and *animus* hinted at in the previous cards – the conscious and the subconscious are now together. At the same time, the arrangement also points forward to Card 19, the Sun, where the same square of materiality frames two figures who are in this case actually touching each other, under the beneficent light of the sun itself. These two young figures under the sun represent developed humanity in its highest phase. The previous card to this, the Moon, figure 194, shows a similar dual group below a celestial influence, but this time the baleful influence of the moon – the mediaeval image of hell – is cast over two howling dogs, symbols of the lower parts of humanity at its most degenerate phase. These three cards – the Pope, the Sun and the Moon – are among the five *atouts* which present a graphic study of influence (figure 208). Clearly, both the extremes of sun and moon (figured in the slouch hat of the Juggler) are meant to link graphically with the Pope card. The Pope is at once the sun and the moon, casting an influence for good or bad depending

THE POPE

86

87

88. 'The Hierophant', as
Waite's version of 'The Pope'.

89. 'The Hierophant', as
Crowley's version of 'The
Pope'. Crowley has
presented his figure
surrounded by the four fixed
signs of the zodiac, as found in
'The World' card.

90. John the Baptist, from
91. Chartres Cathedral. At the
top we see the circular halo, at
the bottom, the circular snake,
who represents the subjugated
demonic forces. Again, top
represents spirit, bottom
materiality.

88

89

upon the attitude of the two people (who are in fact, different sides or potentials of one person) kneeling before him. According to the way this dual figure receives the influence of the teacher, the higher (solar) potentials will be exploited, or the lower (lunar) potentials. Thus, the Pope, seen in sequence, is a commentary on the use and abuse of occult or esoteric knowledge.

The second Arcanum indicates inner and receptive learning; this fifth one indicates oral instruction. The Pope certainly does not represent the querent, who is in fact represented by the duality of the 'active and passive' cardinals kneeling before him, humbly seeking knowledge.

On a deep level, of course, the card relates to the morality of instruction, the right and wrong of instruction, as well as the paradox facing all those who wish for higher instruction: those who seek inner knowledge (wish, so to speak, to bask in the enlightening Sun) must also carry with them the wish for lower things (the wish, so to speak, to live in the hypnotic sublunar world of hell). The card reminds us of what Swedenborg said about heaven and hell – that the spirits dwelling in heaven cannot bear the darkness of hell, any more than the spirits in hell can bear the light of heaven. Each spirit in the celestial world finds its own level in terms of its essential being, just as each embodied spirit in life finds its own level in terms of its essential being and 'vibration'. Specifically, then, the card suggests that we all find the teacher, system, and level of instruction that we deserve! The traditional divinatory meaning of this card is that the Pope stands for duty, conscience, a disposition for the religious life. It is of course linked with Jupiter. The traditional level of interpretation of this card misses entirely the underlying symbolism, and the card is regarded merely as representing a counsellor, generosity, pardon and moral authority. In reverse it indicates a narrow moralist, superstition, a pedant and an incompetent adviser.

Some commentators go to great lengths to indicate that the name Pope (II Papa, in the Italian – figure 84) is connected with the Egyptian god Phthah, for whom the emblem was a triple barred sceptre, and whose responsibility to men was to make hidden duties manifest. Such concepts would link directly with the Pope, without there being necessity for reference to Egyptian deities.

The Pope is sometimes called the Archpriest, Hierophant, High Priest, Grand Master and Gypsy Prince.

90

91

92. *The Italian version of 'The Lovers'.*

93. *Waite's design for 'The Lovers', made in the nineteenth century.*

94. *'The Lovers'.*

95. *An eighteenth century French version of 'The Lovers'.*

92

93

The sixth card is meant to represent decisions and choice, and thus it inevitably links with the duality of the androgyne figure (the two cardinals) of the previous card. A young man stands between two women, as if having to make a choice between them. In the sky a cupid fires an arrow down towards the group.

This image complements and completes the previous one by developing on the important idea of the choice facing the suppliants at the feet of the Pope. The choice operates on many levels, of course, but essentially the decision must be made between activity and passivity, between good and bad, and between such opposing polarities. The two women are obviously the *anima* counterparts of the *animus* figures of the previous Arcanum. The woman on the left is ugly while the one on the right is attractive, and this suggests a conflict or an altercation in the duality of the image. Indeed, the image has been linked with the legend of Hercules, in which the hero is faced with a decision between virtue and vice, obviously in the sense of surrender to basic instincts and external demands. Certainly it is clear that the man in the middle (who represents the querent in certain systems of interpretation) must make a decision between these two opposing elements, if the knowledge he has received (from the Pope) is to be of any value to him. The emergence of a third figure out of what was, in the previous card, two figures is interesting, especially in view of the powerful radiant aura around him. It suggests that in order to understand his inner chaos (to understand the solar and lunar forces in all human beings), it is necessary for man to develop some part within his psyche which will act as an objective observer of his condition. He must learn to see himself. The aura around the cupid in the Italian pack (figure 92) is more openly linked with the lunar and solar disks of the eighteenth and nineteenth Arcana, and in that set more obviously linked with this idea of human involvement in celestial affairs. The cupid within the united lunar and solar disks is meant to symbolize the heavenly parallel of what is being acted out below, when the man makes his choice. What is pristine sun and moon in the heavens has a multitude of dual manifestations on earth.

The stripes of colour on the garb of the observer, of the one who is making the choice between the two women, emphasises that he must make the attempt to find a unity in the plurality which is within himself. The significance of this choice is deepened within a psychological context when we observe

THE LOVERS

·LAMOVREVX·

94

95

96. Contrary to popular
97. belief, witches were not always
old and ugly – even children
were sometimes apprehended as
witches. Ugliness was often
symbolic of immorality,
however, as in 'The Lovers'
card. The broomsticks were
at once phallic symbols and
symbols of materiality, like
wands and staves in the Tarot
designs.

that the left-hand figure may be regarded as representing an older woman (indeed, the mother), and the right-hand figure, the love-object.

Cupid, who may be taken as a symbol of divine inspiration in the context, is directing his shaft towards the beautiful maiden, and the implication is that the man will decide in her favour. This means that he will be compelled or impelled to choose the solar influence, as opposed to the lunar influence. The rather curious gestures of the two women are a little difficult to understand, though their right hands are both pointing to the sexual parts – one towards the man, the other towards herself. We must take it that the image is intended to suggest that the man is being importuned by the women: which is to say that the solar and the lunar influence are both at loggerheads, both attempting to attract his attention. This is of course a fairly precise statement of human condition. If we consider the gestures themselves we see that the man's right hand echoes the posture of the right hand of the girl – the attractive one who represents the solar force. In terms of 'body talk' this means that the man has more sympathy for this particular woman. In other words the man himself is disposed to the solar force, and will be inclined to follow the direction indicated by the divine inspiration above.

In the sequence of this second triad of cards we have seen man fecundated by spiritual forces and made thirsty for knowledge, for an understanding of self: and he is now being pressed into making a decision involving his own inner nature: he must discover a unity in himself, he must make a choice between the sun and the moon, so to speak.

When this card appears in a formal pattern it indicates, at an ordinary level, a need for responsible decisions and choice, benign sympathy and desire, the choice usually involved with matters of relationship. On a deeper level the card is linked with the inner struggle of the initiate to find a centre of balance from which he may make a right decision concerning his future spiritual and physical well-being.

The traditional divinatory interpretation of the card is that the Lovers indicates choice and sensitivity as well as the predicament of the human condition, and it is sometimes connected with the battle between sacred and profane love, as with the Venusian influence itself.

The Lovers is sometimes called Eros, Marriage or Hermes.

97

98. Mediaeval manuscripts showing Apollo as the Sun god. Note the schematic presentation of the horses, which corresponds to that of 'The Chariot' card.

99. Detail of the cupid from Botticelli's 'Primavera' – a common symbol of 'decision in love', 'directed affection' and 'choice'.

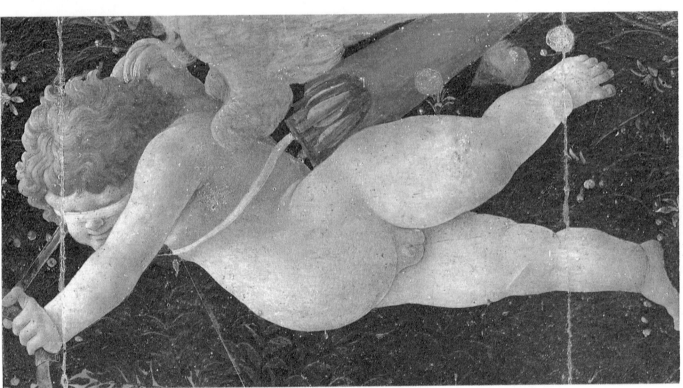

99

100. An Italian version of 'The Chariot'.

101. An eighteenth century version of 'The Justice' card (page 55): a triangle appears to balance a sphere, which shows the designers lack of awareness of the graphic meaning underlying the cards.

102. 'The Chariot'.

103. Graphic analysis of 'The Chariot'. The triadic unity of 'self' (man) should be able to control and direct the spiritual forces (circles) represented by his emotions, which are themselves located in the physical body (the square). The Platonic ideal of man.

100

101

The seventh card, the Chariot, is meant to represent man as he might be, and it is also a commentary on the previous card. The image is that of a prince riding in a chariot drawn by two horses.

The image presents one of the ancient psychological teachings concerning the threefold nature of man. The charioteer represents the mind, or innermost self; the chariot represents the body; and the horses represent the emotions. If the relationship between these three is good, then the driver controls the horses, keeps them in check, and the chariot stays on the road, moving towards some known destination. If the horses (emotions) are not well controlled, because the driver is asleep or does not know how to manage them, then they run off with the chariot and leave the road, running around in circles and going nowhere. If the chariot (the body) is not well built or reasonably maintained, it will break under the pressure of the emotions or under the weight of the driver, and will certainly not stand up to the demands made of it. If the driver (the mind) has no aim, and no destination, then the chariot is moving to no purpose. Thus, a picture of an alert charioteer driving a well-regulated team in a splendid carriage (figure 102) is an analogy of what man might achieve by inner and outer effort in life. The ideal man has perfect development of all his faculties, a sense of direction, controlled emotions, a developed physique and an organizing mind. This is the image of what the Juggler might become if he were to choose the right path and stay with it. The young man of the Lovers is now the charioteer: he has chosen the attempt to contact the solar energies within, at the expense of the lunar energies. Now he has to become aware of what he is himself – a group of conflicting emotions (horses), a severed head (himself as charioteer), and a splendid body (the carriage). This is an image of everyman again.

This card is one of the astrological series, and is governed by the Fire sign Sagittarius. It is no accident that the heads of the two horses are placed where the thighs of the charioteer would be if they were not hidden by the front of the chariot itself, for Sagittarius rules the thighs in the human body (figure 238). The card itself is an allegory of the Sagittarian nature, for it represents man at his highest point of development, and Sagittarius is usually a highly developed type.

Instead of the two columns of different colours which we saw framing the figure of the Pope, we now find four pillars of different colours, suggesting the idea of balance, especially the balance of the four elements within the human body, as discussed on

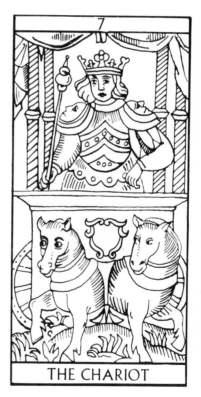

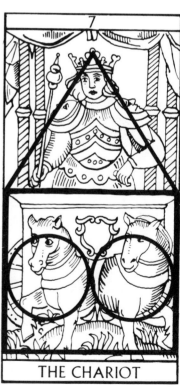

102   103

51

page   . The curious epaulets worn by the charioteer suggest again that the sun and moon of the lemniscate hat in the first Arcanum have been harmonized, and their right places have been found.

The card has been divided into two, a division maintained throughout the first sequence of seven cards. The implication is that the material aspects of life with which the spirit has to struggle, the body and emotions, or chariot and horses, are contained, but now organized, within the square of materiality. Everything has its place, and in some ways this is the most harmonious of all the cards, in spite of its complexity. The ground upon which this chariot runs is less arid than that upon which the Juggler performed his tricks.

Although the two horses are drawing the chariot, they appear to be pulling in opposite directions, so that if the driver (the mind) allows his attention to wander even for an instant, then the passive force of the blue horse will move one way, the active force another, and the carriage will be split in two.

A consideration of the graphic structure of this card will reveal much, for the human figure can be seen as fitting into an equilateral triangle with its base resting firmly on the material square which contains the chariot and the horses (figure 103). This is a fair statement of what man aspires to achieve. The thinking part (the human figure) is in the *akashic* centre of the top square, and the feeling part (the horses) is in the *akashic* centre of the lower square. The 'body' of the chariot binds these two together, just as the body of man links together the head and heart. An understanding of the zodiacal sign Sagittarius is essential in order to grasp fully the implications of this card. On a deeper level, the card stands for that rare human condition, when a state of spiritual dignity prevails and inner desires are in accord with the outer cosmic plane. Is the chariot going anywhere, one must ask when it appears in formal pattern: and if so, where? In a formal pattern for a female querent the Chariot may apply to an unmarried man.

The traditional divinatory interpretation of this card is that it indicates merited triumph over obstacles, success in all enterprises and all Jupiterian influences, such as success in business, talents rightly exercised, progress and journeys by transport. In reverse it indicates the unexpected collapse of a scheme, ill-health and losses.

The Chariot is sometimes called the Triumphal Car, King in Triumph and the Car.

104. Zodiacal circle. Various adepts and interpreters have linked each of the Major arcana with the signs of the zodiac, usually with confusing results. Very often the graphic structure of the cards affords a clue to the real zodiacal association.

104

105. The Archangel Michael subduing Ahriman. Observe the more traditional imagery of the balance – the human soul's worth is weighed against sins. The lower quarter of the panel is set within a square, as with so many Tarot cards.·

106. 'The Justice' card, based on a French eighteenth century set.

107. 'The Chariot'.

108. 'The Chariot' according to Waite. Observe how the change of symbolism – for example, the red and blue horses into black and white sphinxes – has debased and lost the meaning of the original card.

109. The graphic analysis of 'The Justice' shows a link with Taurus, the most materialistic sign of the zodiac. Taurus is ruled by Venus, the planet of harmony and equilibrium.

110. Sixteenth century Italian engraving of a Sybil. The hierarchical pose, and direct symbolism of the sword, is typical of the graphic symbolism which permeates the Tarot card, suggesting that the design of the cards originated about this time, and in Italy.

111. 'The Justice'.

112. 'The World'.

109

110

Card 8　The Justice

The eighth card, the Justice, is meant to represent a warning, and indicates a need for proper deliberation. The image is of a woman holding a sword in her right hand and a pair of scales in her left. She is seated on a throne, and like the Empress she is seen full-face.

Besides the rather obvious connotation of justice, with the scales as a symbol of the equilibrium between good and evil, and the retributive nature of the sword, the card points to the serious need for consideration. The matters revealed in the first septenary have shown ordinary man as he is, and then as he might be – man in control of himself and his faculties – and yet this marks only the first stage in his inner development. Man must stop and consider very seriously if he wishes to continue on this path. The card is one of the astrological series, clearly associated with Libra, and is therefore involved with inner questioning: one of the major difficulties faced by Librans is that of coming to decisions. In very simple terms the card may be understood as an image of the psyche deliberating on what action must be taken.

Each of the first seven cards shows a figure holding something in the hand which determines the nature of the following cards within the septenary. In the first group we see the development of the baton into a sceptre, and in this second group we shall see the sword develop upon the theme of the difficulties and struggles facing the man who chooses the path of inner development. The sword is a form of the cross (page 122), and the cross is considered in terms of representing materiality, restriction and a burden.

The form of the card is based on an oval, which contains the whole body of the female, with a crescent, formed by the throne, balanced on top of the oval (figure 109), which in itself must be linked with the circle of spirit, as it so clearly is in the twenty-first Arcanum (figure 112).

The presence of this card in a formal pattern for a male querent usually indicates a woman to whom he will be attracted: the figure is full-faced, and therefore not distracted by others.

The traditional divinatory interpretation of the card is that the Justice indicates equilibrium, regularity, order and tranquility, and it is linked with the influence of Venus. It indicates stability, conservation, reason and the law. In reverse it indicates complications, timidity, lawlessness and injustice.

The Justice card is sometimes called the Judge, Astraea, The Scales and Magdalene. The card is sometimes called *Ma*, after the Egyptian goddess of Truth, an image of which was worn by chief judges.

JUSTICE

111

THE WORLD

112

113. 'The Wheel of Fortune'.

114. A Hermit, from a mediaeval manuscript.

115. The 'Rosy Cross' from a rosicrucian manuscript. The seven layers of petals represent the harmonious meeting of the law of three (trinity) and the law of four (elements) which permeates the Tarot symbolism.

116. 'Adam and Eve' by Durer. The four animals at the foot of Eve symbolize the four elements in harmony before the Fall of Man.

117. 'The Hermit' who is
118. moving to the left, associated with the past.

114

116

The ninth card is perhaps the most simple of all the *atouts*, for it veils almost no other deeper esoteric meaning than may be applied to the idea of 'searching'. The thing for which the Hermit is searching may be determined only from the relationship it holds within the formal pattern, which is why this is an extremely difficult card to discuss in isolation. It is an image of an old man searching in the dark, feeling his way with a stick (the most recurrent of all single symbols in the Major set), and lighting up his path with a lantern.

It is significant that the Hermit is facing to the left, for this area is associated with the past. Since we read from left to right, we tend subconsciously to associate the right-hand side of a picture with the future, and the left with the past. This is why Goya so frequently makes the left-hand side of his dismal etchings the lighted area, and allows threatening groups of soldiery or the like to 'block' the future (figure 123), suggesting the loss of all hope. Emphasis on the past is what concerns the Hermit: perhaps the suggestion is that being an old man, he has little hope for the future, but this thoroughly materialistic view of life is not in accord with the spirit of occultism which sees hope in death. The preoccupation with the past must be what is symbolized by this card: it points to the fact that the past may be a weight which will pull down even the blithest of spirits. In the Italian pack the Hermit actually carries a sack, which emphasizes this sense of the weight of the past. The presence of the card in a formal pattern always points to a need for liberation from some memory, in order that the new, the future, may be embraced.

The sense of weight in this card is very strong for other reasons. The cape and body of the Hermit give the impression of being compressed into a square of materiality. This idea finds particular emphasis in the Italian card (figure 13), for in this the red activity has been stamped over the cape and body in a form which only slightly diverges from that of a square. The hat of this hermit is red, suggesting that more effort is required with the head – more creative thinking must be established: preoccupation with the past, apparently a pleasant and harmless way to relieve present responsibilities, may become a dead weight that prevents the spirit digesting present experiences, and thus may ultimately restrict spiritual growth.

The Hermit may suggest the idea of search, but it may also be taken as a clear indication that the querent must change his attitude to something for, consciously or not, this attitude is blocking his

Card 9 The Hermit

THE HERMIT

PAST

117   118

119

spiritual progress. In this sense, therefore, the card is quite rightly associated with the astrological Saturn, which governs limitations, as well as fixed attitudes, and the conservative emotions of fear and denial. The presence of the card calls for a general 'opening up', a serious need for expansion to counteract the inherent sense of frustration and limitation.

In popular cartomancy the Hermit is associated with the urge to withdraw from life, and of course with spiritual questioning. It has sometimes been associated with the idea of social death, on the basis that those who are engaged upon the 'inner path' feel little desire for the mayic world of illusion. This is a typical misunderstanding of the nature of the so-called inner path which, in the west at least, requires a healthy exchange with, and love of, the material world. Perhaps the nearest we can get to such a meaning within the framework of this card is for us to note that the Hermit is using his stick to support himself, and feel his way, whilst the Fool is using it confidently in his march forward. The card is supposed to indicate silence, meditation, withdrawal, study and concentration, though the grounds for such traditions are difficult to grasp from the original *atout* form. In reverse it indicates avarice, an unenquiring personality, and misanthropy.

The Hermit is sometimes called Prudence, Capuchin, the Old One, Truth and the Sage. To those commentators who believed that the Tarot pack was derived from the Egyptian originals, this Hermit card presents something of a problem. For example, van Resselaer has to admit that 'the meaning assigned to it, and its value for soothsaying, hardly corresponds with the personage depicted, so it is supposed that the artist who modernized the ancient design has altered it too completely to be recognised by those unaquainted with the original intention . . . the attributes or values given to the card rather quarrel with the design, for they signify friendship, protection, and wisdom.' The Hebrew *Teth* of the Italian pack certainly confirms this idea of protection, for it represents a roof, or a place of shelter, and may be linked with wisdom and forethought. In this connexion we may discover some validity in the idea that the card represents the Greek cynic philosopher Diogenes having emerged from the tub in which he lived (again the idea of protection) and searching for an honest man. With such associations we may more properly see the way the card links with wisdom, prudence, sympathy, and with the desirable qualities in a friend.

120

121

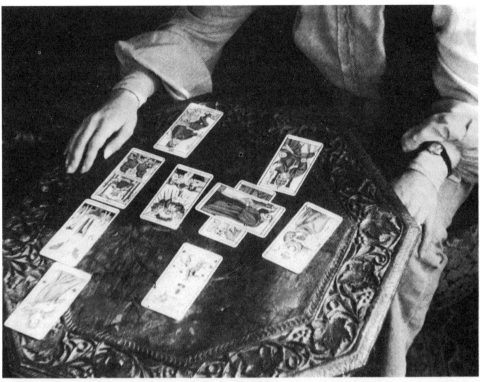

119. *A formal order being used for a Tarot reading.*

120. *An Italian version of 'The Hermit'.*

121. *A Rosicrucian image of a hermit, moving into the future.*

122. *The formal pattern is dominated by 'The Hermit' card, always an indication of strong inner search.*

123. *Goya's aquatint from 'The Disasters of War' which illustrates how the right hand side of the picture, representative of the future, and therefore of hope, may be cut off, and become an area of threat.*

FUTURE

123

124. An Italian version of 'The Wheel of Fortune'. Note the eight spokes.

125. A mediaeval wheel of Fortune, with a hierarchical figure sitting in judgement, and human beings ascending and descending.

126. 'The Wheel of Fortune', a kind of bestial mockery of the mediaeval imagery.

127. The ouraboros snake, from an alchemical text. This is the snake which must be overcome, if spiritual development is required.

124

125

The tenth card is meant to represent certain conditions of experience in the ordinary world, and it does this by adapting to its own purposes the familiar mediaeval image (figure 125) of the turning wheel which at one point lifts man up, at the next throws him down. The image in the Marseille Tarot shows two similar figures clinging to a turning wheel; above, on an unmoving pedestal, sits an allegorical beast, a kind of crowned simian sphinx, clutching a sword in its left front paw. The Italian Varello version differs in many important respects: the ascending form on the wheel is bestial, the descending figure is partly human, while the figure on the pedestal above the wheel is a king, clutching a sword and wearing a crown. It is one of those rare cases where one must admit that the Italian card is more subtle than the French pack, for the essential meaning of the card is involved with the idea that anyone who believes in the phenomenal world of experience will remain half human and half bestial, forever caught in rising and falling through a series of lifetimes which are linked through *Karma* with each other. The presence of a king seated in splendid isolation points to the occult teaching that man may become a kind of spiritual god by learning, through suffering and through spiritual disciplines. He must leave the turning wheel and sit above life, in a spiritual realm where he is no longer conditioned by fear, the prime moving force of ordinary life and the emotion opposite to love, the moving force of spiritual life. The circle, then, symbolizes spiritual fear and the isolated figure symbolizes love, though the complex image also sets out the conditions of ordinary life which the inner search reveals to be so intolerable. It is a world of illusion and change, growth and decay, and its controlling force appears to be impermanence, its only 'destiny', decay.

The basic dual polarity which lies behind the structure of our material universe is expressed by the ascending and descending creatures, though we must understand that at the centre of every wheel there is a still point upon which the hub turns. The point is invisible and an intellectual abstraction, but it is an important occult teaching that although the material world appears to manifest in dualities, we may only understand the interpretation of the spiritual and the material if we think in terms of triads, by introducing an invisible third force. The seated figure is the material embodiment of the person who has succeeded in reaching this still point of the turning world, entering into the dot within the solar glyph (figure 127), and emerging reborn from the material world into the celestial world of spirit – a

Card 10 The Wheel of Fortune

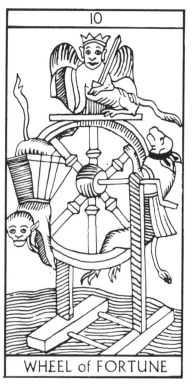

126

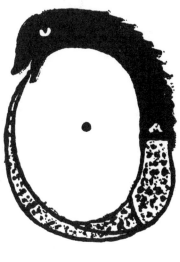

127

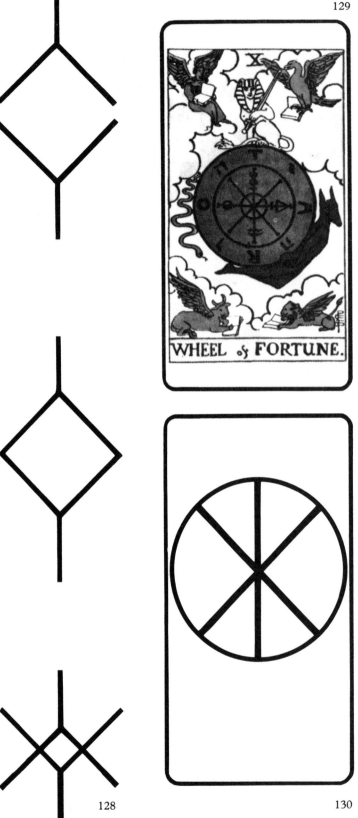

theme commonly enough described in alchemical treatises. It is possible that the simian nature of the forces is emphasized because these suggest the imitative faculties in man, indicating through the symbols that in the ordinary world old ideas are continually being presented in new guises, personalities are always built up on a framework of learned responses, and everything within the scope of human endeavour appears to depend upon the ability to imitate. Cirlot suggests that the apes are symbols of the dark powers in man.

Jean-Marie Lhote has listed very intelligently many of the problems to which the images of the Tarot cards give rise: one of the problems is involved with the fact that the Wheel of the French pack has only six spokes, when it should have eight. This is not a problem when seen as a graphic device by which a deep philosophical idea has been incorporated into the structure of the card. The six-angled cross formed by the spokes of the wheel is of very ancient origin, in fact, and was probably a pagan sun wheel, though it has been taken by some scholars as being a Christmon of I (Iesus) and X (Christ) (figure 128). A deep level of real significance may be traced if we examine the two component forms from which it is constructed. First we have a fork which represents the arms of man reaching up towards the heavens, token of sun-worship, of spiritual aspiration, or of prayer.

The same sign inverted expresses the idea of grace descending from the skies: this is the graphic symbol of the hand of God, as well as a symbol of grace bestowed or offered.

When the two signs meet, they represent the spiritual kiss of God, and when man and God meet, an inner space, which is an image of the dot, a centre of spiritual growth, is formed.

As the two forces intersect, the union is complete. A six-pointed star is formed, and the yearning for union is completed. The structure suggests that just as grace cannot exist without God, God cannot exist without man. The new figure radiates outwards in a display of life and strength, and is therefore a fitting symbol of solar life and motion. It is for this reason that it is used in the Wheel of Fortune. The tendency for those living in the world (which is a product of the meeting of spiritual powers and material powers, both springing from the yearning of man for God), is to get involved with external show and consequently forget the inner and invisible power of the central hub, from which the movement itself arises. This is perhaps why the hub of the wheel is red, pointing to an active source of life, or to a need for an active search for the still point around which God and man eternally revolve. The inner half of the spokes is blue, the vertical supports of the wheel are yellow, suggesting a meeting of passivity with spirituality, which must be yoked together at the centre through activity. The outer white half of the wheel must be considered as being separated from the inner central hub and the radiating blue inner wheel.

The solar-glyph interpretation of the wheel is not possible with the Italian pack, which has seven spokes, was very possibly intended to have eight, and is certainly of a different colour system. Perhaps this is because in the earliest Italian Tarot (the Visconti pack) the Wheel is derived completely from the mediaeval image of the turning wheel.

If we turn to the French card for explanation of the strange creature above the turning wheel, we are thrown into some confusion. The figure appears to be aping the Empress of the third Arcanum, for it has wings, is full-faced, and carries a sword over its shoulder. We may deduce that the curious figure is meant to show that in life the aping of spiritual achievements is only too easily undertaken – the knowledge of esoteric truths may be used exoterically, for the benefit of the material ego, in a form which is ultimately a mockery of truth.

The traditional divinatory meaning of the card indicates a period of instability, change and impermanence. It is linked with lunar-mercurial change. The card is sometimes called The Fortune, Osiris, Fate, Chance, Tarot and Rota. Within the pseudo-Egyptian system we find that the god Osiris is sitting in Judgement above the wheel, with Anubis climbing up and Typhon descending. In terms of occult understanding, however, we must link the circle with the urge of the Luciferic forces, which require men to become pure spirits, and the spokes with the Ahrimanic forces, which require men to become pure animals. True man must find a point of balance between these two forces, and within this central point he will be able to establish his freedom. The larger part of occult wisdom is concerned with the struggle between these two forces, which from the earthly standpoint must be regarded as being evil in that the spirits both require man to become like themselves – at the expense of his freedom. It is perhaps only in the light of this occult tradition that the truth concerning such dangers as drugs and the 'guru' systems which are sweeping the Western civilization may be properly understood, and the terrible dangers to Mankind and to individual man be heeded.

THE EMPRESS

128. *The interpretation of the trinity of God and the praying trinity of man gives rise to the six-spoked wheel.*

129. *'The Wheel of Fortune' according to Waite.*

130. *The basic graphic form of 'The Wheel'.*

131. *The hierarchical figure presiding over the wheel is graphically linked with 'The Empress' card.*

132. *The Indian Ada-Nari, whose four arms (holding symbols of the elements), and head and body give the six polarities of the wheel.*

132

133. 'The Hanging Man'.

134. 'Strength'.

135. The Death card.

136. The personification of 'envy' by Giotto (Scrovegni Palace). The amazing symbolism of the snake emerging from the mouth, representing the negative Mars, of astrology, is precisely that contained in 'The Hanging Man', which represents Man upsidedown.

137. 'Strength'.

138. The curious gesture, and the lion mouth, represent the lemniscate of Sun and Moon.

133

134

135

136

The eleventh card is meant to allegorize on one level transmutation, and another level the triumph of intelligence over lower forms. It is an image of a woman gently forcing open the mouth of a lion. She wears a hat reminiscent of the Juggler's slouch hat in the first *atout*, which was intended as a meaningful lemniscate, symbolizing the union of sun and moon. It is a humanized verson of this meeting which is portrayed in this present card.

The lion symbolizes the sun: a frequent image in alchemical texts is that of a lion attempting to devour the sun (figure 142). The female symbolizes the moon, and we see in this struggle a prefiguring of the sun and moon of the eighteenth and nineteenth cards (see page 100). The fact that this level of interpretation is intended, and is implicit within the structure of the card, may be seen from the curious position of the woman's arms and the lion's mouth, for these together form another lemniscate. Taken all in all, this female card is the logical extension of the Juggler card, descriptive of the time when the Juggler himself begins to pay attention to the world around him. The allegory is fairly clear: we see a firm gentleness and a higher quality of energy (confirmed by the shape of the hat), and subjugation of a lion, which must be a symbol of wild energies and brutal forces – indeed, of the emotions themselves – and we must not forget that the Leo of the zodiac, symbolized by a lion, rules the human heart, and by extension the emotions. The allegory has been linked by some Tarot commentators with the idea of Virgo vanquishing Leo – even though no such zodiacal tradition exists! The nearest thing in astrological doctrine is that Virgo is regarded as the sign of service which 'organizes the chaos which the creative Leo frequently leaves behind'. Perhaps the card may be interpreted on this level. Certainly the idea is clear that the woman is controlling the lion, and not destroying it – echoing the alchemical idea that base matter and lower forms of energy cannot be destroyed, but may be refined. It is an age-old occult truth that one must not attempt to change or destroy something because it is distasteful, but rather attempt to put it in its rightful place or transform it.

Curiously enough, the female does not have to exert any great effort to open the jaws of the lion (the lemniscate of sun and moon 'happens', as it were). We must therefore assume that the title of the card does not refer to the female principle, but to the male principle pictured as a solar lion. The lion is submitting to this treatment: he is not struggling to get away as he might easily do, and thus the image

Card 11   **Strength**

STRENGTH

137

138

139. Wood engraving by William Blake. The tension in the figure arises from the fact that the Sun shines on the tree from the left, but on the Moon from the right.

140. The evolution of the lemniscate hat of 'strength'.

141. Waite's version of the 'Strength' card.

142. The lion devouring the Sun, from an alchemical text of the seventeenth century. There is an astrological link between such a concept and the idea of the serpent in Giotto's 'Envy' of figure 136.

139

140

STRENGTH.

141

suggests something which is 'against nature'. The woman stands as a manifestation of some eternal power which is encouraging the lion to go against its own nature, in order that something in the lion may change: the aim is to transmute some of its bestial nature into a quality of spiritual love.

The presence of this card in a formal order is always a sign that something within the framework of the question may be transcended, that something of an inferior quality of energy may be transmuted into a higher form. The card demands that attention and effort be put into the situation, towards this end of transformation.

The assimilating of the sun, or the Leo principle of the Lion, into the human being is expressed through many different diagrams within the occult and alchemical systems (figure 142, for example). The card of *Strength* goes further than merely depicting a struggle with the Sun of Leo, and shows how the struggle is involved with the Sun and Moon, in the lemniscate contained in the graphic structure of the card. The integration of Sun and Moon, in 'pure spirit' and 'pure materiality' as figured in the circle and cross of astrological glyphs, and indeed in the basic astrological diagram (figure 173) as well as in the wheel and spokes of the previous card, are clearly linked with the struggle between Lucifer and Ahriman, as revealed in the previous card. Without the struggle between these evil forces, life as we know it would not be possible, and yet, as this Strength card proclaims, we must struggle to make use of Lucifer and Ahriman – pure spirit and pure materiality – in order to develop our individuality and freedom. The Strength card, and this freedom finds expression in the wholesome development of the human ego. Whilst living in a body (caught in the samsaric turning of the wheel) it is not possible to be entirely free from the Luciferic forces or from the Ahrimanic forces – but it is necessary to learn how to deal with these. This the card symbolizes by presenting the female of spiritual freedom grasping in her hands the Moon and the Sun, in a struggle to transform both. Such ideas, which have been devolved to a rather arid level of understanding in modern psychology, under such phrases as the integration of the conscious with the subconscious, is expressed in many great works of art (figure 139, for example) in which the tension between Lucifer and Ahriman are symbolized through the relationship between the Sun and the Moon, the Sun representing all that is pure spirit, the Moon representing all that is pure materiality. The card is sometimes called Force, Fortitude and Neith.

PHILOSOPHORVM.

& sicca soluantur, calcinentur, siue sublimentur se
cundum quod viderit, & melius iudicatur secun
dum sanum sensum operantis.

142

Ich bin der war grün vnnd guldisch Löwe ohn sor=

143

Card 12　The Hanging Man

The twelfth card is one of the richest symbols in the Tarot pack, and it is not surprising that it has caught the imagination of twentieth century painters and poets. Its symbolism deals beautifully with the problems of the human condition which our way of life is intensifying. The card has been interpreted in many different ways, and certain of these interpretations are contradictory in meaning: there is little doubt, however, that this *atout* is a commentary on man's inner state in relation to ordinary life. It is an image of a man with his hands tied behind his back, hanging by one foot from a simple gibbet formed by two leafless trees and a crossbar.

Man is pictured as hanging in space, his isolation reflecting his basic loneliness, and the uncomfortable posture reflecting his own inner torment. It is interesting to note that the man does not appear to show any pain, in spite of his posture – in the Italian pack he shows no concern, as though unaware of his position, while in the Marseille pack he is actually smiling. This is, of course, a fair statement of the attitude of the majority of people to their inner world, for they do not realize their own inner chaos, or the chaos of the world outside (the inner and the outer being interdependent), and in spite of the torment in which their spirit dwells, they show little real concern.

The subtle graphic structure underlying this card deepens the sense of hopelessness connected with the human condition. The head and arms of the Hanging Man together form a triangle (figure 146), which is why the hands appear to be folded or tied behind his back: the apex of the triangle is pointing downwards, suggesting that the world of the spirit, the trinity, is in disarray and chaos. The blue legs of the man are crossed, implying that materiality (the cross of matter) is weighing down the inverted triangle, and we observe that the legs are clad in red, implying that the weight of the material cross is actively engaged in keeping the triangle in this position.

In order that we might understand the deep significance of this cross we must examine two aspects of graphic symbolism. The cross may be seen as the meeting of four lines, figure 42, in which case it is held in the esoteric tradition to be the meeting of the four elements of Earth, Air, Fire and Water, joining to produce the central point of life, the fifth *Akashya* (see page 23). Alternatively, the cross may be seen as two lines crossing each other, like a crucifix, with one line representing the horizon of the earth, and the other (descending) line representing the spiritual descent into matter. It is

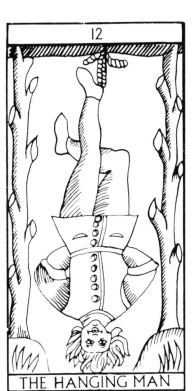

THE HANGING MAN

144

143. A seventeenth century scheme of the alchemical redemption of man. Observe that the Moon is turned away from the sun, symbolic of the state of guilt in man, since subconscious mind (moon) cannot face the conscious mind (sun).

144. 'The Hanging Man'.

145

THE WORLD

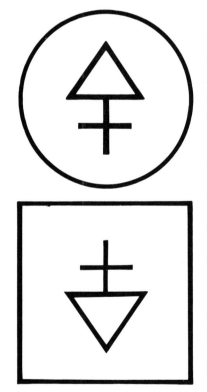

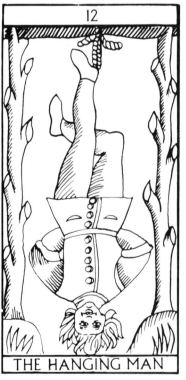

12

THE HANGING MAN

145. 'The World'.

146. At the top is a diagrammatic analysis of the graphic significance of 'The World' card, at the bottom an analysis of 'The Hanging Man'. The two cards are graphic opposites.

147. 'The Hanging Man'.

148. Judas, aided by a devil, hanging himself as a result of the betrayal.

146

147

specifically to this latter cross that the twelfth Tarot card applies. The horizon line is used in an astrological horoscope to indicate the polarity of selfhood (the Ascendant first house) and relationships to others (the Descendant seventh house, sometimes called the house of marriage).

The vertical line shows the ascent and descent of the spirit; it marks the polarity between heaven and hell, which is why in the crucifix figure we find the INRI scroll at the top, symbolic of the Word, and the skull at the bottom of the cross, symbolic of hell, which is matter devoid of vivifying spirit. If we link this Christian symbolism with the twelfth Tarot, we find that the human head is in the place of the skull, proclaiming that the state of the Hanging Man is virtually that of death. This deep teaching is favoured with some hope, for the graphics insist on a relationship between the hair of the man, which is depicted as hanging downwards, and the few shoots of grass on either side, implying that life may emerge even from this 'human death'.

The graphic structure of the hanging figure has been widely recognized by cartomancers, but the significance of the containing square which frames the figure has been largely ignored. As we have seen already (page 23), the square is itself an arrangement of the four Elements which are bound in the fifth invisible element of *Akashya*; thus we have to consider the inner hanging figure as being linked with the invisible life force.

On this level of interpretation we may see that the card proclaims that man as an invisible life force is upside-down, that human life as it is now being lived is somehow unnatural. At the same time, the structure of the card reflects upon the freedom of man to remain in this uncomfortable position, for he is to a certain extent free of the four elements which bind him into the temporal experience: this is why the rope which connects him to the topmost of the four elements, the horizontal bar, is not actually tied to his feet: man is hanging from nothing!

The traditional divinatory meaning of the card varies enormously – by certain schools it is held to indicate 'death through violence', yet by others it is supposed to represent 'voluntary sacrifice': it indicates selfishness for some schools, and triumph over flesh for others. In reverse it may refer to things as varied as 'unfinished projects', a 'thief escaped' and even 'suicide avoided', and such nonsenical epithets as low-level commentators would wish to place on this remarkable symbol.

A real grasp of its significance must take into consideration the graphic symbolism, as well as the

70

fact that tradition links it with Judas Iscariot. In the
Charles VI pack the Hanging Man has two bags of
(presumably) gold or silver in his hands, which
inevitably suggest the biblical thirty pieces of silver,
and the mediaeval tradition that Judas hanged himself shortly after his betrayal of Christ. It is on such
grounds as these, as well as on the grounds of the
underlying graphic structure, that occultists have
been prepared to link this card with the zodiacal
sign Scorpio. It is certainly interesting to observe
that the card finds its graphic opposite in The World
atout, Arcanum 21 (figure 145), which shows a woman
standing, her head and hands arranged in a triangle,
her feet crossed, and her entire figure surrounded by
a spiritual circle! This 'reversal' of the Hanging Man
is interesting, for it really depicts *anima mundi* (page
109) triumphant. Her living garland (compared
with the lopped dead trees which enclose the hanging
figure) is a testament of life spiritual, and the entire
mandorla is supported by the four fixed signs of the
zodiac (figure 145), which are the living spirits of the
four elements we saw confining the hanging figure.
If we see the four elements which frame the man,
and which actually participate in making his posture
so uncomfortable, so miraculously changed into the
spiritual hierarchies, then we must presume that the
condition of being a hanging man must be necessary
for the evolution of *anima mundi*, for the spiritual
development of the world. The procreation of
Taurus, the creativity of Leo, the inner striving of
Scorpio and the humane objectivity of Aquarius,
may all find fulfilment in man only when he has been
prepared to realize his own loneliness, and to see the
crisis in human affairs, a crisis which is perpetual.
This is why on an ordinary level we must read the
significance of the card as relating to an inner crisis
that needs an inner decision; why on a higher level of
interpretation we may regard the Hanging Man as a
sublime statement of a cosmic truth, that man must
die to be reborn on a higher plane.

The Hanging Man is sometimes called Balder,
Judas, the Judas Iscariot, the Thief, the Tau Cross
and the Place of Sacrifice. It has been suggested that
this last appelation, linked with the number 12,
might connect the card with the twelfth house of the
zodiacal figure – the house of *karma*, where the sins
of life are stored in preparation for the cleansing fire
of post-mortem experience, a cleansing which,
although unpleasant, is necessary before a new life
in a body is possible.

148

149. The cross links the four elements.

150. The sanguine temperament of the Air element.

151. The flegmatic temperament of the Water element.

152. The choleric temperament of the Fire element.

153. The melancholic temperament of the Earth element.

154. The death card.

155. The crossed arms and the curve of the scythe echo the glyph for Saturn, see figure 158.

EARTH

FIRE ──┼── AIR

WATER

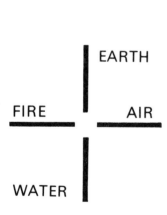

149

150   152

SANGVINEVS · 1·

SANGVINEI·FRONTIS·DICVNTVR·IMAGINE·LÆT·
VNDE·VOLVNT·HILARES·SÆPE·VIDERE·IOC·

COLERICVS ·2·

TRISTES·AT·COLERA·SVNT·HI·QVI·SEMP·ABVNDANT·
FORTER·EFFECTV·QVE·MOVET·ONME·SVO·

FLEGMATICVS ·3·

FLEGMATIC·NVLLAS·IN·MENTIS·ACVMINE·VIRES·
IDCIRC·MERITE·NIL·QVOQ·LAVDIS·HABENT·

MELANCOLICVS ·4·

AN·MELANELICI·STVDIVM·SINE·FINE·PERERRANT·
HAC·GENERIS·CELEBRES·PRE·FVERE·VIRI·

151   153

The thirteenth card of the Tarot pack is the only unnamed card in the *atout* set, though it is popularly called the Death card, and is linked with the zodiacal sign of Capricorn. It is probably this zodiacal rulership which accounts for the fact that the skeleton representing death is clothed with skin around the arms and pelvic area, for the sign of Capricorn rules the skin as well as the skeletal system of man. This cadaver image of death is well in accord with the mediaeval tradition, like the dancing figures from the *Nürnberg Chronicles* (figure 159), which may have been designed or cut by the youthful Dürer. The figure is a wasted cadaver, as may be seen in the flesh colouring of the whole, in the right arm, in the skull, and in the fact that there are still tendons on the thighbones. This marked attempt to portray decomposition may be taken as a sure indication that the card is concerned not exclusively with death, but with a state of transformation and change. For this reason, if for no other, those cartomancers and designers who have presented this thirteenth card as a pure skeleton (figure 156) have lost much of the meaning contained in the original.

The graphic symbolism of the card is interesting. The skeletal frame is in the form of a half circle (see figure 154) which represents spirit in a state of tension, the idea being that a crescent on its back will act like a saucer and hold spiritual energies safely (as in the horned crescent of Mercury – figure 49), whilst a crescent upside-down, as in a dome, will allow spiritual energies *to run away to waste*. A crescent standing upright, as in this thirteenth card, is in a state of tension, for it may fall either way – it therefore has the potential of spiritual gain or total loss. The graphic structure suggests a pull between good and evil forces. Beneath the crescent there is a curious structure, for the hands and arms of the cadaver form an awkward cross with the handle of the scythe, indicating the idea of a material cross. Underneath this cross, and attached to it, we find the crescent shape of the scythe blade. In mediaeval manuscripts, and even in later printed books (figure 157), a cross mounted on a half circle was the sigil for Saturn, clearly representing the cross of materiality (which we examined at page 23) weighing down the semi-circle of potential growth.

The card points to the need for control, since it is evident that which way up the crescent falls will mark what happens to the energies represented by the card (see diagram 155). The crescent is already leaning over and threatening to fall in an inverted position. The iconography of the card suggests death, and the underlying graphics suggest a strong

154

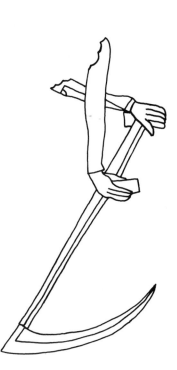

155

156. The Italian version of the death card.

157. Putrifaction, from an alchemical text. In the black star to the upper right is an early version of the glyph for Saturn, consisting of a cross of matter weighing down the semi-circle of spirit.

158. The Death card, with its graphic equivalent.

159. The dance of death, probably designed by the youthful Dürer. From the Nuremberg Chronicles.

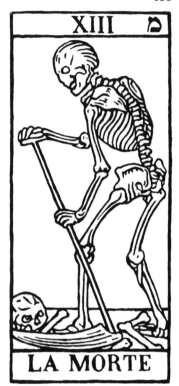

XIII

LA MORTE

157

tension – perhaps upon one level a hint that death is the earthly equivalent of the resolution of the tension between spirit and matter. Alternatively the significance of the symbolism may suggest that a tension should be reduced by some willing sacrifice.

It is not unnatural that this card should be regarded as an ominous portent by querents who know little of its underlying symbolism. It is important therefore that when this card emerges in the formal pattern, its true significance be pointed out, perhaps by indicating that on an esoteric level the card deals with change, the need for transformation and effort. The image of death is used only because this represents a particularly strong example of transformation, when what is invisible and important in man is removed temporarily to the invisible sphere which is its proper domain. Rakoczi maintains that it is as well to gloss over this card when it appears in a formal pattern, for even an explanation of the 'real' meaning of the card, with all the attendant qualifications, is usually insufficient to put the average querent at ease. I cannot agree with this: my experience confirms that the presence and significance of the card must be fully explained if the real force of the Tarot response through the formal pattern is to be understood.

Two very interesting deviations from the normal 'death' image are significant: the figure is scything towards the left, and he has unwittingly chopped off his own right foot. The direction of scything is what accounts for the link with the sigil for Saturn, which would not have emerged if the figure had scythed to the right. The amputated foot may be seen on one level as indicating that even death has no complete dominion (i.e. death will destroy even death), but on a more significant level we see that had the leg continued downwards it would have formed a strong cross with the handle of the scythe, and would have spoilt the clear graphic symbolism of the figure.

Scatterings of hands, heads and bones on the black earth, with the sprouting grass of blue and yellow, reaffirm the general interpretation above, and form conclusive proof that the image is not intended to be one of the 'great leveller'. The destructive element, which is represented by the crescent shape of the scythe blade, is red, suggesting that the destructive force is in fact active and purposive in its implications. The allegory is clearly a link with the idea of Saturn pruning the tree in order to rejuvenate it; this, as Cirlot points out, is paralleled by Siva who transforms beings by destroying their physical form without damaging the essence. The destruction of form, dematerialization, is an essential part of purification – room must be made for the new, and here we have an image of death marking a point of transition. Looked at positively and from a heathen spiritual point of view, the card is clearly a sign of rejuvenation, whilst from a negative point of view based upon fear, it is the sign of dissolution, the ending of a finite thing or project.

At the bottom of the card we find two heads, on the left that of a woman, on the right, that of a king. These two refer to the moon and the sun, which are found at the top in crucifixion paintings. Their placing at the foot of the card indicates the concept of spiritual and cosmic entities laid low, as well as the inversion of an separation between the *anima* and the *animus*.

The traditional divinatory interpretation of the card is that Death indicates transformation, unavoidable death, and the Saturnine influence in general. It marks transition above all things, and in particular relates to the 'metaphysical death' which is associated with disillusionment in the sensible world of appearance. Tradition holds that in reverse it indicates such things as moral suicide, opposition to projects arising from external sources, and fatality in general: obviously the graphic structure completely denies such a traditional interpretation of the reversed card, for it lends a Jupiterian cast to the card (see diagram 76), and leaves the sun and moon (the two heads) in their proper places.

The Hebrew *Mem* associated with this card (figure 156) means fertility and the urge towards formation and development, suggesting that the card is more linked with regeneration than with Death in the sense in which it is commonly understood. Death in the astrological tradition is linked with Scorpio, with the house of death ruled by Scorpio, and yet the significance of this sign and house is rarely correctly understood. In esoteric astrology, we must understand that all ideas are conceived in Aries, struggle with form in the materiality of Taurus, and find expression in the Air sign of Gemini. When for some reason or another the Aries force of pure spirit cannot struggle through the form of Taurus to find expression, it is deflected by Taurus to the far side of the zodiac, to Scorpio, the region in which it must remain *until it is regenerated*. It was on this level of understanding that the role of Scorpio and the role of death was understood by the ancients: it is on this level that we must understand it when we deal with the Tarot pack.

The Death card is sometimes called Time, the Skeleton and Azrail.

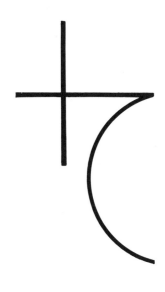

Imago mortis

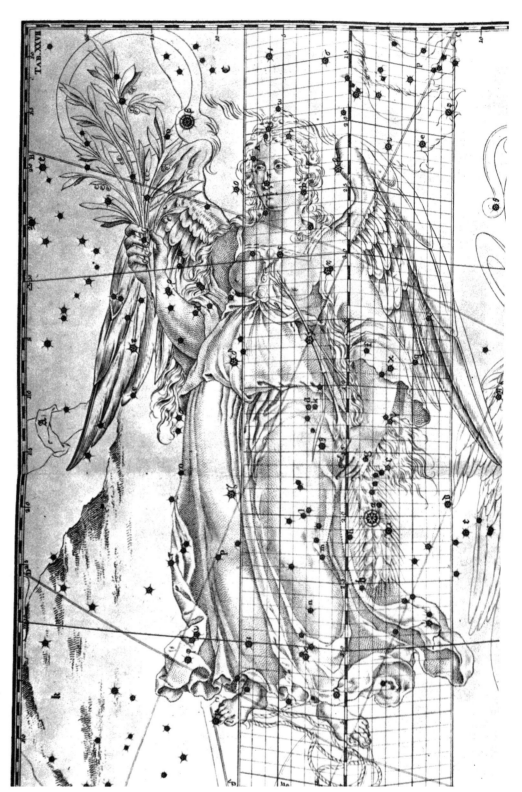

160. The astrological image
of Virgo, the attractive young
girl carrying can, and with
bared breasts. This traditional
image of the sign has been
occluded in recent times, in
favour of a hard and barren
maiden, which bears no
relation to the astrological
truth concerning this sign.

161. The French and Italian
version of 'Temperance';
these are very similar in the
important aspects of the card.

160

The fourteenth card is linked with the Death card in that it presents a statement of the *positive* aspect of the destruction/rebirth cycle. The image is one of a winged woman clothed in a flowing garment, who is pouring water from one cup into another.

This card has been explained in many ways, though the majority of explanations are quite unsatisfactory. The figure is not gynandromorphous, as several writers maintain, for it is clearly female in the form usually depicted. The distribution of colour – the red sleeves and the wide division of the entire robe into two halves of red and blue – indicates that the two polarities of activity (red) and passivity (blue) are to be read into the figure, and it is probably this which has resulted in the dual-sex interpretation. The position of the blue and red jugs recalls the Chinese sigmoid *yin-yang* circle (plate 52): a white dot in the black area suggests that there is no passivity without activity and vice versa, and similarly here is a red jug on the blue side of the figure, and a blue jug on the red side. The curious position of the arms and shoulders, and even the placing of the jugs, suggest a rotary movement strikingly evocative of the moving *yin-yang* figure. In alchemical terms the figure allegorizes the *conjunctio oppositorum*.

The act of pouring must be linked with the idea of transforming energies – passive energies (from the blue jug) pour into the active receptacle (the red jug): not a drop is spilled, suggesting the ancient idea of the circulation of energies, regeneration and the perpetual flux of life. The currents of liquid add a refinement to this idea of eternal flux, for the streams are three at the commencement, just above the red half of the dress, but two only above the blue half of the dress. Clearly, the idea expressed in graphic terms is that active creation springs from a triadic action (the Christian trinity being one of many examples), but manifest itself in nature (blue passivity) only in dualities, since the third force is always invisible to sublunary creatures, according to the ancient occult tradition. Although all manifestations are essentially triadic, it is possible for us to perceive only the duality of negative and positive forces. Such a teaching is developed in alchemical sources and has found a modern counterpart in the ideas expressed by many modern occultists and esoteric writers, notably Ouspensky in his *In Search of the Miraculous*.

It has been suggested that the pouring of water from the blue to the red jug denotes the transformation of energy as it passes from the lunar order (blue) to the solar (red). Thus, energy of a transient and emotional nature is changed to energy of a fixed and

Card 14 **Temperance**

TEMPERANCE

LA TEMPERAN

161

162. Detail from Raphael's 'Crucifixion' indicating something of the esoteric depth underlying the chalice symbolism of the 'Temperance' card.

163. Virgo ruling the stomach of the zodiacal man points to the significance of spiritual rebirth associated with the 'Temperance' card.

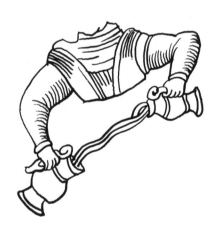

162

intellectual nature – the passage of subconscious energies into a conscious expression is the whole nature of creativity.

The presence of wings on any figure in a mediaeval design always suggests spirituality, and for this reason alone it must be regarded as forming a strong nodal force at any place on which the card falls in a formal pattern. The card has been linked with various zodiacal signs – surprisingly enough, Hades for example relates it to the sign Aquarius. There can be little doubt, however, that the winged Temperance is, iconographically at least, linked with Virgo, the young maiden of astrology, who used to be depicted with wings and holding sheaves of corn, one pointing up, the other down, as in the example from Bevis at figure 160. The concept of Virgoan selfhood is involved with a critical assessment of material facts, in order to arrive at truth. It is on this level that the card must be understood.

The traditional divinatory interpretation of the card is that Temperance denotes the uniting of opposites, discipline and self-control, and it is linked with the solar-lunar influences, probably because in some packs one goblet is silver (the colour of the moon) and the other gold (the colour of the sun). It indicates a voyage safely completed, and sociability. In reverse it indicates a lack of personality, lack of control and general corruption.

In the Pseudo-Egyptian system the card is linked with *Nut,* who is depicted as a guardian of the shades of the dead, and within this framework of reference it is possible to understand the Hebrew letter *Nun* (figure 161) associated with the card, for this signifies fruit and all things which are produced. One of the ancient methods of divination, which was involved with pouring oil on water, and studying the results, has been associated with this Temperance card. Perhaps however, we need not go back to the oil and water cups of the Babylonians to understand the spiritual significance of this card: the detail of the angel recovering the blood of Christ, from the famous Raphael crucifixion at figure 162, suggests an interesting iconographical connexion, for the upper chalice is collecting the blood given in a spirit of free self-sacrifice for Mankind, whilst the lower chalice is collecting blood taken in an act apparently of cruelty, again pointing to the idea of the uniting of opposites. The passage through body, chalice and water flow (figures 161) links with the Chinese *yin yang* symbol, as well as with the turning Wheel of Fortune.

Temperance is sometimes called Isis, the Great Mother and the Queen of Heaven.

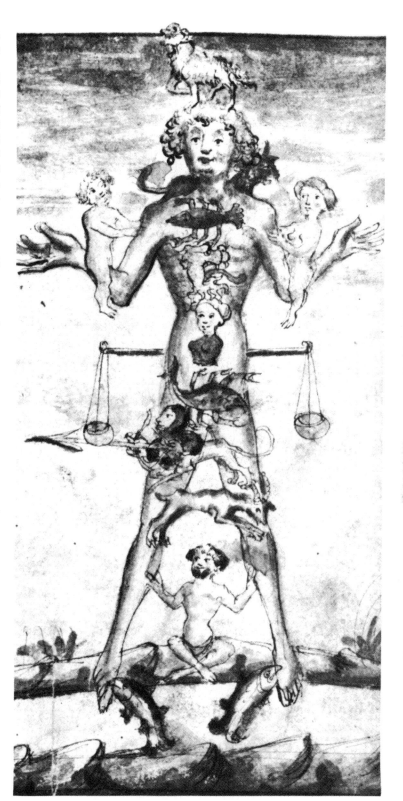

163

164

164. *The circle protects mankind from damnation: in the astrological system, as in the Tarot, the circle represents spiritual forces.*

165. *The mirror on the wall, in which the maiden sees the behind of the devil, is circular in a graphic mockery of the spiritual circle. It is this kind of mockery which the graphic structure of 'The Devil' (figure 167) contains.*

166. *'The Devil'.*

167. *The graphic significance of 'The Devil' mocks, by distortion, the circle, and also the popular image of macrocosmic man, who has always his private parts in the centre of the circle in which he stands (see figure 170).*

165

Card 15 The Devil

The fifteenth card is meant to symbolize the idea of stagnation which often manifests in material life as a sense of complete frustration, as a total barrier to spiritual freedom, moral development and even physical liberty. The image is one of the Devil standing between and above two chained slaves.

It is very difficult to separate the image of this remarkable card from all the nonsense which has been written about it, and it must be admitted that almost all the original force of the symbol appears to have been lost to us, even though the strong connexion with alchemical sources, both iconographical and ideological, is evident (figure 166). The figure of the devil in this card has been identified variously with Pan, Baphomet of the Knights Templars, and Lucifer himself, though it is evident from a study of the images that it is meant to represent the lower force, inertia and slavery in everyman. The blue wings and legs indicate the essential passivity and 'weight' of the figure, and the posture of his hands is almost certainly intended to echo the Juggler in the first Arcanum, with one hand pointing towards heaven and the other pointing down towards earth, grasping a broken sword, thus clearly linking this figure with everyman.

The figure is hermaphrodite, for there is a penis and developed breasts, but it is also half bird and half animal, as the wings and extremities testify, so it is safe to assume that the image is meant to convey all the lower characteristics and qualities of man, his animal desires, his passivity and his preoccupation with sex; the significance of the red girdle around his belly was discussed on page 21. The visual associations with the Juggler suggested by the posture of the hands would indicate that this is an image of the part of man which cannot be developed, the part which man must carry with him while he inhabits an earthly body.

The two figures standing below this image of the devil are clearly meant to echo the two figures in the fifth, sixth and seventh Arcana, and are therefore a further reference to emotions and energies which have either not been developed or are not capable of development. It is frequently pointed out that the Devil incorporates into his being the four elements of the material world: the blue legs represent Earth, the blue wings, Air, and the red hair and horns, Fire. Indeed, some claim that the green scales on his body in certain Tarot packs represent an undine nature, and therefore Water, but these are not found in the original cards, and once more we are faced with the fact that the earlier packs were of wiser design than the 'restorations' and inventions of later

THE DEVIL

THE DEVIL

166

167

minds. Water is the missing element precisely because this is the element which loosens and dissolves, and the whole point about this card is that it represents a rigid state of being, incapable of being dissolved: it needs refreshing with the element of Water. It represents Earth without the fortification of Water, which would relieve its parched condition and permit life to emerge. Stasis is slavery, and permits no freedom to make decisions – the only hope it holds out is for a change of attitude. The design of this fifteenth card may be usefully compared with the design of the Chariot, Arcanum 7. The precise symbolism of the horns on the three figures is hard to grasp, as is the significance of the tails of the smaller figures. Several ancient traditions maintain that developed and perfected man – that is man before the Fall – had horns and a tail, but it is difficult to link this idea with the card itself, unless we see it as symbolizing the tyranny of the Devil of selfhood over the real, pre-Fall and perfect man, who was in perfect four-fold elemental harmony within himself (see page 109), and therefore in harmony with the world. The aim of the allegory is to represent the forces of stagnation and regression, and it could be that the forms themselves are meant to suggest potential growth – for, as Cirlot has pointed out, the first two signs of the zodiac are themselves supposed to be based on horn symbols. It is this suggestion which links most forceably with the graphic structure underlying the card, which suggests a rather elongated symbol for Taurus, the most material of all the zodiacal signs. The lower part of the circle is easily traced in the ropes which curve in from the necks of the captives, the upper part – completed by the curve of the shoulders and arms of the devil. Arising from this elongated circle – a symbol of spirituality which is superficially out of place in the present card – is the half crescent of the wings (figure 167). It has been suggested that the graphic symbolism of this card is rendered more meaningful if considered as resulting from the superimposition of two structures. The lower half of the card is the square of materiality, formed by the bodies of the slaves, the bottom edge of the card, and the imaginary line joining the heads of these creatures with the private parts of the devil (figure 169). Above this square of materiality we find an inverted triangle, the apex at the devil's penis and its base formed by the line of the top edge of the card. This latter graphic analysis represents the world in disarray, along the lines of the analyses provided for figures 58 and 59. We see that the spiritual promise of the first graphic structure is completely weighed down by the square of matter and the inverted triangle. The message is, however, that even the materiality of the devil is within the domain of grace. The image of the devil, standing within a circle, with his sexual parts at the centre (figure 169), may be regarded as a parody of those mediaeval images of cosmic man, such as the famous one from Fludd (figure 170).

The strong sexual connotation of these two graphic analyses – especially the last one, which suggests that man's spirit is off-balance because it pivots on sex – is emphasized by the three distinctive half circles which dominate the card. The curve of the wings contains the breasts and represents the spiritual urge, the wish to fly. The curve of the lower part, marked out by the binding rope or chains, represents the forces which keep men earthbound: this curve contains the iron ring which holds man to the lowest part within himself. Linking the two, we find that curious red girdle which echoes the two curves and yet remains in the dead centre of the card, indicating that the uncontrolled force of sexuality ties man to the devil and prevents him flying.

The traditional divinatory interpretation of the card is usually histrionic, because the esoteric significance of its images has been missed: usually the Devil indicates disruption of character, loss of power and money, and the domination of animal lusts. It is linked with the Martian and badly-placed Venusian influences, and because of this is usually taken in reverse as indicating intrigues and weakness of character. The truth is, as the previous analysis indicates, the card represents a period of stagnation, complete frustration and a sense of an insuperable spiritual barrier.

In the esoteric tradition the Devil is said to have rule over the domain of Scorpio, which in turn rules the private parts of the human body. This partly explains the graphic structure of the card, but it points also to the significance of the Scorpionic domain as outlined on page 75. Scorpio is the 'stagnant water' which symbolizes all those incompleted intentions, half truths, lies and frustrations which entered into the physical world of Taurus, from the pure spirit of Aries, and yet were not able to manifest freely in Gemini. Such half materializations remain in this domain of Scorpionic hell, awaiting regeneration by sacrifice or through suffering. All crimes, all deficiencies of spirit, are contained in this Scorpionic domain.

The Devil is sometimes called Satan, Baphomet, Lucifer and the Master of the Coven.

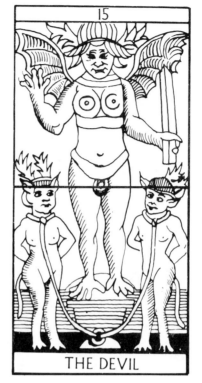

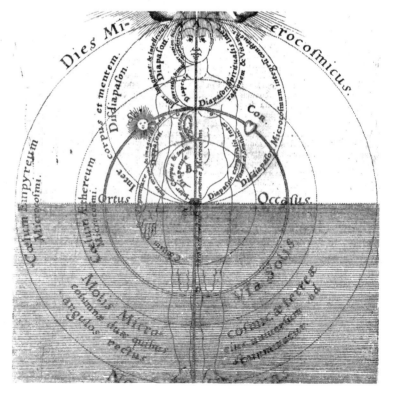

168. *Black magic, involved with the worship of satanic forces, is the use of cosmic forces for personal aggrandisement: it is therefore by no means the exclusive concern of witches . . . It is to this selfishness that 'The Devil' of the Tarot refers.*

169. *The division of the card emphasise the fourfold materiality, which is in the form of a square below – in a cross, formed by the wings and arms of the Devil, above.*

170. *Macrocosmic man, from Robert Fludd's* Cosmi Utriusque.

171. Crowley's version of 'The Devil'.

172. 'The House of God'. A circular turret on a square tower.

173. The horoscope is in a sense an example of the 'impossible' squaring of the circle – the circle represents pure spirit, the cross pure materiality. The improbable union of these two forces is the human being.

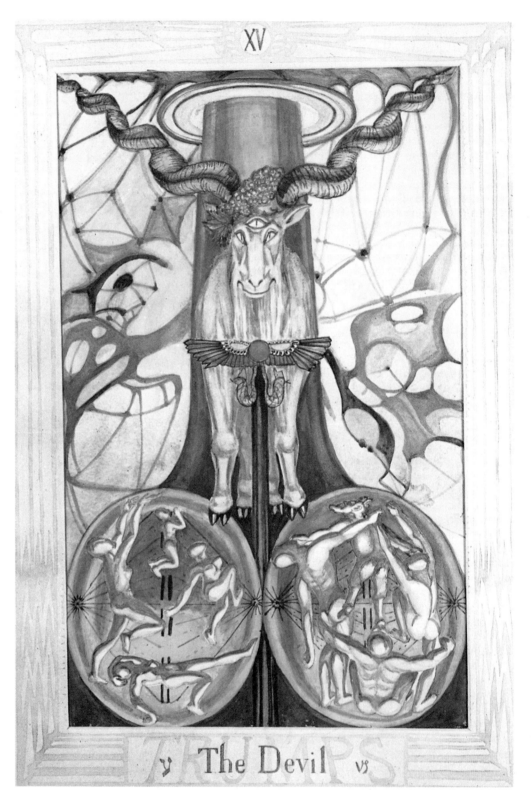

171

The sixteenth card has always presented something of a difficulty for commentators who, for obvious reasons, usually take it as signifying catastrophe or illness. The image is of a tower being struck at the top by lightning, with two men falling from the tower; in the sky around the tower are red, white and blue dots like hailstones.

The traditional name for this curious card, the House of God, is almost as much of an enigma as the card itself, and the tendency in England has been to refer to this image as the Tower Struck by Lightning. In the Middle Ages, however, 'House of God' was the popular name for a hospital, and whilst it is at first sight difficult to reconcile this title with the content, the flesh-colour of the building may indicate that the entire structure is supposed to stand for the human body; the lightning flash striking off the castellated tower may be taken as implying that man's head (i.e. his reasoning faculties) are affected to such an extent that he is physically or mentally ill. This level of interpretation becomes more insistent when we realize that the shaft of the building is clearly indicated to be square, but the tower above it is circular: this links both with the idea of the impossibility of squaring the circle, and with the idea that the battlement tower, though now removed by the lightning flash from heaven, did not fit the walls of the edifice in any case. The head of man, which is to say the seat of the intellect, is portrayed as divorced from his body and his physical needs. The lightning is therefore merely sundering two elements which did not harmonize, and which may to all intents and purposes be regarded as separate. Many occultists are of the opinion that the intellect has reached its maximum development in man, and that in future incarnations it will be other organs, as yet undeveloped in ordinary beings, which will be used as instruments of perception and communication. The separation between mind and emotions, between head and body, is the basic force underlying the contemporary tragedy of the loss of spiritual quality, and the general insanity of the modern view of man and his relation to the cosmos. On this level, then, the lightning flash may be seen as a catastrophe which forces an important issue: the circle cannot be squared, so let the circle and the square be separated to live their own lives. We may apply this to the image of man individually, in terms of body and mind, emotions and mind, or to man in terms of relationships, or indeed to particular social conditions as we consider appropriate.

We are fortunate in that there have survived from the past two or three mediaeval images which are

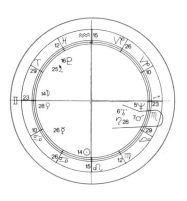

HOUSE of GOD

172

173

174. *An Italian version of 'The House of God'.*

175. *The formal pattern used for Tarot interpretation in a combination of a circular distribution of cards (reflecting the horoscope structure) and a fourfold linear distribution, which may be associated with the squaring of the circle.*

176. *Illustration to the Golden Legend. Reims Cathedral.*

XVI

LA TORRE

clearly the iconographic source for this sixteenth card, such as figure 176 a detail from Reims cathedral. The image refers to the story in the Golden Legend which tells how, after the Holy Family fled from Herod and finally set foot on pagan territory, whenever they entered a town, the pagan temples and altars tumbled down – presumably because the spiritual vibration of the holy three was too great for the *genius loci* to withstand. This esoteric teaching may be applied with considerable practical value to the card when it appears in a formal pattern, the implication being that the querent has not been able to respond with sufficient 'being', with sufficient understanding, humanity or spiritual vibration, to a particular circumstance or set of circumstances, with the result that his inner or outer world has been shattered. Certainly, the presence of this card in a formal pattern indicates that something surrounding the querent has been damaged, though it is something (a building, within the symbol) which may be rebuilt – neither of the two human beings in the *atout* are, as yet, damaged. The warning implicit within the card is that if a new fabric is to be erected, then one should take care not to attempt to place a round turret on square walls!

Even without the help of the Golden Legend, we may understand that the tower is itself a symbol of height, and by extension a symbol of spiritual development: within this framework alone then, the image of a tower being destroyed, with human beings falling from it, must of necessity point to a general disaster affecting the subject. The coloured 'hailstones' are difficult to understand, but their spherical shape implies that the difficulties spring from the querent himself, rather than from an external source: this is because the sun is *radiating* droplets, and the moon is *sucking* in droplets (figures 202 and 203), indicating a direction of force. In this card there is no direction of force, so we must presume that it comes from within.

The traditional interpretation of the card is that it indicates catastrophy, excess, disaster, and the pursuit of chimerical ideas, and it is linked with Martial influences. Sometimes Jupiterian influences are assumed, because it is Jupiter who handles the lightning flash. In reverse the card is taken as indicating sickness, misdirected punishment, and the loss of freedom. It is linked by tradition with the story of the Tower of Babel: the link is a tenuous one, though of course both stories express the same subconscious state from different points of view.

175

176

177. An Italian version of 'The Star'.

178. Danby's 'Deluge' – the four elements of Earth, Air, Water and Fire which also appear in 'The Star' card seen here warring. Observe that the Moon is full, yet separated from the Sun by only a few degrees – this 'impossibility' is presumably intended to heighten the strange drama of the scene.

179. 'The Star' as designed for Waite.

180. 'The Star'.

181. The human face is at the centre of the four elements.

177

179

178

The seventeenth card is meant to symbolize inspiration, creativity and the spirit of humanity seen as a creative force. The image is of a naked female pouring water from two pitchers into a stream. Above her head is one larger star surrounded by seven smaller stars. In the background is a green tree upon which a bird is perched, suggesting the idea of the soul resting on the Tree of Life or the Plant of Knowledge. In later editions of the card the tree was (almost inevitably) transformed into a flower, and the bird became a butterfly.

The fourteenth Arcanum depicted a woman pouring liquid from one jug to another, but the woman under the stars is pouring her liquid on to the earth and into a stream, suggesting the idea of nourishing and creating. The jugs in this card are again blue and red, symbolizing the interchange of creative forces, and the blue water suggests a malleable materiality which is the raw material of creative art. The positioning of the pitcher in the woman's left hand, covering her pudenda, is a clear association of the creative energies with sexual energies. The presence of the two trees in the background emphasizes the idea of growth, and the bare breasts reiterate the idea of nourishment.

It has been suggested by some commentators that the small stars represent the Pleiades. This idea would introduce the nature of Taurus, and there appears to be no strong reason why the suggestion should be taken seriously. Indeed, the precise relationship between the stars and the figure is hard to determine – perhaps the implication is that the creative forces are heaven-born, and that the artist, in breathing life into form, is doing on a microcosmic level what the stars are doing on a macrocosmic level. The graphic suggestion is that the stars and planets quicken inert matter, and that the resultant force, which is man, should in turn inject inert matter with life through making works of art.

However, the card is named in the singular, not in the plural, and it is to the single fixed star Sirius which the image refers. The star is of the first magnitude, now in 13 degrees of Cancer, and to the ancients its heliacal rising marked the Dog Days, the hottest period of the year.

The heat associated with Sirius is important in this present context, for the Star card, which has been described as the 'most gentle and agreeable of the Tarot', combines in perfect harmony the four Elements of Fire, Earth, Air and Water, and it is on this level of union and harmonious combination that the card must be interpreted in a formal pattern. The Fire is symbolized by the presence of Sirius, the

THE STAR

THE STAR

180   181

182. The relationship
183. between the hair, arms,
jugs and water recalls the
sigmoid yin yang *diagram,*
the circular movement of which
reflects the cosmic struggle
between light and dark
principles.

184. Diagram showing how
185. the cards of a formal
pattern (figure 175, for
example) have a circular
motion which is concentrated
into one single card, a kind of
static lens which bring to a
focus their individual forces.

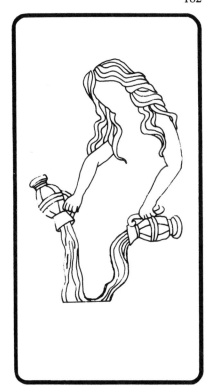

Air by the bird in the background. Fire and Air combine harmoniously, for Fire requires the oxygen of Air to keep it alive, whilst Air seeks the warmth of the flames to make it more rarified, more able to ascend to the heavens. This is why the Fire symbol and the Air symbol are both found in the topmost half of the card and it is very significant that the human face is in the centre of the card.

Earth is of course symbolized by the ground itself, just as Water is symbolized by the pool at which the naked woman kneels: these two elements are contained in the lower half of the card, as is fitting, for in the alchemical tradition both Water and Earth sink, while Fire and Air rise. The trees growing in the background symbolize the union of Water and Earth, for it is the function of water to soften and refresh the dry earth and make it fructify, while it is the function of earth to lend water a channel or depression by which it may take on a shape or identity of its own. These four harmoniously disposed elements surround the human figure, which is itself in the esoteric tradition supposed to be composed of all four elements, plus the invisible fifth of *Akashya* (see page 23). Her head is placed at the very centre of the card, suggesting the idea of the four elements revolving around in some cosmic order. Within the context of the *five* elements, the card hints that what is most important in the human figure (the central head) is in fact quite invisible, because it is identified with the fifth invisible element. Certainly the spirit is invisible, both in man and in works of art: and we might echo the words of the fox in his last advice to the Little Prince: 'Remember, that which is most important is always invisible!' The graphic structure of the card lends a sense of circulation to the card, with the flow of water from the pitcher representing the lower part of a circular movement, the arms and shoulders representing the upper motion (figure 181). This suggests that the human being is investing the four elements with a specific life of their own, enhancing the *Akashya* element, so to speak – which is another way of describing creativity. Again, the circulation from water to human being may also be taken as symbolizing recurrent rebirths – incarnation followed by a period of reintegration within the cosmic waters – that is, individuation in the human body punctuated with release into the world of spirit, which is so often symbolized as a running stream of water. The general harmony and balance of the five elements in this card recalls the esoteric teaching which claims that before the Fall of man, the four elements were harmoniously balanced within all human beings, with the result that there was no sickness, no fear, no disbelief: all human beings loved and were incapable of fear. It is perhaps a direct intuition of this truth which has led so many commentators to regard this card as the most spiritually promising of the pack.

The traditional divinatory interpretation of the Star is that it indicates inspiration, creativity and contact with someone who will inspire the querent. It is linked with the solar and Venusian influences. In reverse it implies bad luck, an uneven flow of emotions and even mental illness.

When the *Yin Yang* form of the female (figure 181) is clearly grasped, it will be seen just how clearly this links with the dragon snake Ouroboros (figure 183) who is often depicted half-black, half-white, to represent the eternal cosmic struggle between Lucifer (the white of pure spirit) and Ahriman (the black of pure materiality). Man may be represented as the midpoint of these two forces, and so once more we see man caught up in the eternal circle of the four elements, two of which are centripetal (Earth and Water), seeking to stand alone, yet needing each other, and two of which are centrifugal, seeking to rise up in individuality, yet needing each other. Thus the drama of the universe is enacted upon around man, who stands at the akashic centre of this display. Such a diagram of man standing at the midpoint of the fourfold display is found in the horoscope figure of the squared circle we studied in the House of God (figure 173), and it is also bound up in the formal pattern by which the cards may be manipulated to study the situation which gives rise to a question. The first six cards of the so-called Celtic pattern (see figures 185 and 258), represent the querent (a crossed pair of cards) surrounded by the four houses of the horoscope. The one on the left symbolizes the selfhood of the Fire sign Aries; the one on the right the relationships of the Air sign Libra; the one above the crossed pair symbolize the aspirations of the Earth sign Capricorn, whilst the one at the base represents the commencement of the Water sign Cancer. In such analogies of these, which arise from subconscious depths, and through clairvoyant perception, we may observe the remarkable fecundity and valid interpenetration of all the occult systems, even when they have been preserved imperfectly, and when they are not fully understood by the modern linear mentality.

The Star is sometimes called the Dog Star, Destiny, and – among the more imaginative cartomancers – The Star of the Magi, for reasons which are difficult to grasp.

184

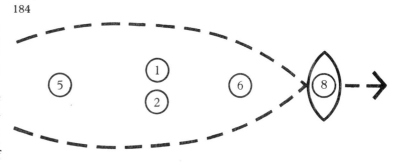

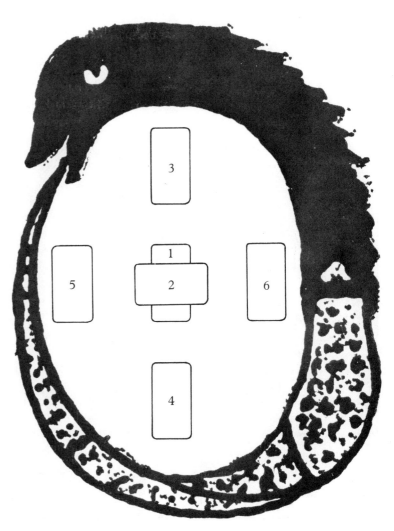

185

186. 'Hecate' by William Blake. The male and female forms press in on either side of Hecate, to suggest a graphic connexion with the alchemical 'union of opposition' which occurs so often in the Tarot designs.

187. 'The Moon'.

188. 'Hell' by Martin. The heat represents only one side of the traditional image of hell . 'The Moon' card is associated with the cold, isolationist side of hell.

187

188

THE SUN

189. *The image of soldier's asleep round the tomb is an esoteric commentary on man, who is 'asleep' in his higher being. The Judgement card refers to this inner stupor.*

190. *'The Sun' observe the direction of the influence 'tears', and compare these with those in 'The Moon' card.*

191. *'The Judgement' – the grouping of figures round the tomb contains a similar message to that in Blake's 'Hecate' opposite.*

192. *'The World'.*

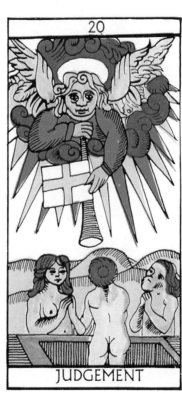

JUDGEMENT

THE WORLD

189

191

192

193

The eighteenth card is meant to allegorize the conditions of hell. It is an image of a moon over a landscape with two castles, two dogs and a crayfish in a formal pond. The setting depicts the conditions of the lowest level of the spirit in the material world. The light of the moon is reflected from the sun, and it is a passive body, which is why it is depicted as a blue disk, surrounded by red, white and blue rays. The landscape below is a ghostly yellow, suggesting the dim lunar light, and the two dogs baying at the luminary represent the human emotions drawn to the moon, fount of imagination and magic. That the moon is sucking up energies from the earth is indicated by the shape of the tear-like droplets converging on the moon from below, for they are pointing in the opposite direction to the ones in the next card, where they are evidently being projecting downwards by the sun. The lunar influences are not creative – they suck people dry through imagination and evil involutory forces, reminding us of Ouspensky's vision of the moon as representing the lowest and heaviest material form. The dogs (human emotions symbolized seem to be strangely compelled to the moon, yet are frightened by its influence, perhaps barking a warning at what they fear. The water and crawling crayfish are a direct reference to the Cancerian nature of this card, for the Cancer symbol is the crab, and Cancer is of the Water element and ruled by the Moon.

The most obvious thing about this card is something more than the individual component symbols, it is the strange almost surrealistic atmosphere of the whole card, which, in its Chirico-like tensions, portrays the final agony of the soul in hell. This is certainly the most frightening card of the entire set; as Cirlot says, it is 'pregnant with negative and fatal significance'.

In the occult tradition, the sun and the moon are intrinsically bound up with the inner world of the human psyche. At death the vital spirit returns to the sun, whence it came, and the soul must return to the moon, where it remains invisible, 'divested of the light of the vital spirit'. This is why Eliade is able to write, 'The idea of the journey to the moon after death is one which has been preserved in the more advanced cultures . . . It is not difficult to find . . . themes of the moon as the Land of the Dead or as the regenerating receptacle of souls . . . This is one reason why the moon presides over the formation of organisms, and also over their decomposition (as the colour green). Its destiny consists of reabsorbing forms and of recreating them . . . Hence, for Plutarch, the souls of the just are purified in the moon, whilst

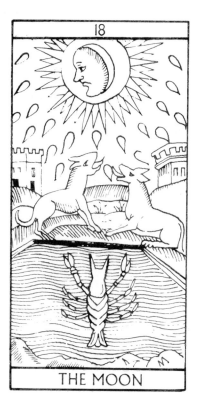

193. 'Endymione asleep' by Cima da Conegliano. Endymione represents humanity sleeping away life under the influence of the Moon.

194. 'The Moon'.

194

La Lune.

195

their bodies return to earth and their spirit to the sun.' The conditions of flux which relate to the inconstant moon in life are therefore projecting into death, and the moon itself becomes a fitting symbol of what is mutable and transitory – this is why many pictures of the Virgin Mary and the *anima mundi* show her standing or sitting above the crescent Moon, symbolic of the triumph of eternal spirit over the mutable (figure 210).

But if the human spirit is influenced by the moon *after* death, how much more so (according to tradition) is it influenced by the moon during life. All material fortunes are supposed to be determined by the fluctuations of the moon, and this tradition is so obvious that it need not occupy our attention here: it is sufficient to say that it is possible to study the general life pattern of people from their horoscopes in terms of the path which the moon traces in its symbolic progress through the horoscope in the days immediately after the day of birth. A more important idea, not unrelated to the idea of the moon as the Land of the Dead, requires examination at this point. The ancient Greek myth of Selene and Endymion points to this idea on a psychological plane. Endymion was a beautiful young shepherd, with whom Selene fell in love as she looked down from the skies. So great was her wish to possess the object of her love that she decided to put him to sleep, and during his period of slumber to lie with him. Endymion is obviously humanity, kept asleep (spiritually speaking, of course) by the force of the moon, that the moon might take her pleasure. The idea of humanity being in thrall to the moon is psychologically interesting. Perhaps it is literally true that human beings are spiritually asleep because of the influence of the moon – it is certainly true that the subconscious (always symbolized by the moon) is separated from the conscious mind (always symbolized by the sun), and it may well be that the Greek myth was an attempt to present this psychological truth in story form. The opposition and conjunction of sun and moon, with all attendant implications, is frequently referred to in the graphic symbolism of the Major Arcana.

The spirits, or the spiritual forces, are being sucked up into the moon, symbolic of the idea of human spiritual forces being used up in a transitory round of activity. And yet this curious moon face is contained within the circle of the sun – a fact scarcely noted by the majority of writers on the Tarot! This hints both at the moon's dependence for its existence on the sun, and also at the need for a reconciliation between the subconscious (moon) and

96

the conscious (sun) – perhaps the aim of all healing, of all religions, and of all artistic endeavours.

These legends are themselves sufficient to suggest that the benign face of the moon, that symbol of growth and femininity, has a dual nature, and so it is not surprising that in ancient times the ruler of dual Cancer was represented by two goddesses – the celestial Diana and the infernal Hecate (figure 186). In the glyph for Cancer we may see the celestial Diana as the lower part, 'the mild and gentle queen of night', the crescent which will enable the seed of spirit to grow; the infernal Hecate, that giant of a woman, hair formed from snakes, a sword in her hand and a voice of thunder, accompanied by the baying and howling of dogs, is the upper, uncreative half of the glyph. It is surely this Hecate who rules over hell, over the hidden face of the moon! The need to be creative, pay homage to the spirit, and fight inertia, is symbolized in the Moon of the Tarot in a negative way, with the Hecate-side emphasized by the stagnant pool, baying dogs and sucked-up spirit.

The appearance of this card in a formal pattern must always be regarded as a warning of some kind – very often it refers to excessive imagination or pernicious influences: even to drugs or alcoholism, depending upon the structure of the question. In some cases the Moon may refer to the instability of the querent in regard to a particular set of circumstances connected with the question. The associations and myths touched upon in the analysis should be sufficient to suggest lines of interpretation, but it must be kept in mind that the card always refers to a kind of hypnosis or state of sleep, the nature of which the querent may not understand even when it is pointed out to him.

The occult significance of the card is quite clearly involved with a description of the human condition should the human impulse fall prey exclusively to the dominion of the materialistic force of Ahriman. The pure aridity of this promise is horrific.

The traditional divinatory interpretation of the card reflects these associations with the moon, for it is held to predict perils and dangers of an unforeseen nature, lack of security and a dangerously strong imagination. Needless to say, it is linked with the lunar force. In reverse it is supposed to indicate deception, flattery and false assumptions.

The Moon is sometimes called the Card of Dreams, Ast the Serpent and Hecate.

LA LUNA

THE MOON

197

195. 'The Moon' card from the tarot pack of Charles VI.

196. An Italian version of The Moon.

197. Waite's version of The Moon, which looses all the original force of this disturbing card. The Scorpionic association with the eighth house hell has disappeared and lunar herself is virtually benign. The waters in which the crayfish lives no longer appears to be stagnant.

198. 'The Sixth Palace of Hell' by Fay Pomerance. Lileth, who in the occult division was the first wife of Adam claims sleeping man for her own at the point of death.

199. The evil face of The Moon from the three headed Mercury of the alchemists (see figure 74). In the occult division The Moon is a malignant force connected with materiality.

200. 'The Sun'.

201. An early French version of 'The Sun' card.

199

The nineteenth card is meant to allegorize the conditions of spiritual growth, and in this respect it stands in complete opposition to the qualities represented by the previous card. It is an image of the sun burning down on two semi-naked children in an enclosed garden: the sun is the creative fount of life, the male principle, the creative urge, the way of the spirit, the vivifying source which enables matter to act as the vehicle for soul and spirit: it is the invisible force behind all life. The card depicts the conditions of rebirth and development which will lead to one of two things: a renewal of the old condition prior to the loss and degredation set forth in the previous card; or a new way of life, in which creativity and love of life become purposes in themselves. It is no accident that the Sun and Moon cards should be adjacent in the Tarot order for, as we have seen, the idea of the sun and moon in conjunction produces the important lemniscate symbol (figure 203), which represents the circle of life, from sleep (lunar) to waking (solar), from bad (lunar) to good (solar), from death (lunar) to life (solar), as well as all other earthly rhythms of being. Because of this connexion, the two figures beneath the sun, which are often wrongly associated with the Geminian twins, must be linked with the two dogs baying at the moon: these are the human versions of the degraded canine souls – their nakedness, and extreme youth suggests the biblical idea of souls waiting to be reborn, or given life. Perhaps the most important point is that they are at least touching (which is to say, relating), so that the loneliness of the human condition symbolized by the separated dogs under the moon is mitigated here.

The wall behind these figures is clearly intended to enclose the space in which they are standing, and we must remember that the Persian root of our own word *paradise* meant 'an enclosed space'. The containing area is meant to form a clear contrast with the rather frightening open and surrealist landscape beneath the moon, and it introduces the idea of the growth of the spirit in the womb – an idea paralleled in the ancient astrological symbol for the sun, which is a single dot (a seed) within a circle, with all the attendant sexual and spiritual connotations.

The posture of the two children is, according to some commentators, meant to recall the strong force of the Gemini symbol which relates to the duality of creativity and destruction. The sun is bestowing light equally on both these forces, and the rays are obviously emerging from the sun and influencing life below. The sun's rays are red, blue, white and yellow – all the colours in the cards save green – implying that the sun is the source of everything,

THE SUN

200

201

THE MOON THE SUN

the divine and active source of life and energy, giving rise to the dualism of life below. The rays of the moon are droplets (souls, perhaps?) being sucked into the lunar deadland, while the rays of the sun are droplets thrown out in creative joy, perhaps the souls of those to be reincarnated, or the 'souls' of ideas which will be used for creative purposes by the humans below.

The sun itself has always been a symbol of renewal in its daily 'rebirth', while the moon has been a symbol of impermanence and decay, mainly because it waxes and wanes in its cycle. This kind of attitude to the luminaries has given rise in some cultures to the idea of the sun representing the eye of God and the moon, the evil eye.

It must be emphasised that the occult significance of this card may be understood only in regard to that of the previous card. Whilst the Moon symbolizes the extreme force of the Ahrimanic compulsion to mere bestiality and towards materialism, the Sun card symbolizes the extreme force of the Luciferic compulsion towards spirituality. The moon, so to speak, floods us with the waters of desire which dissolve our human form, whilst the Sun dries us up, and withers our human form. Within the occult teaching we see man as an entity which must wrestle with these two forces, so frequently symbolized as the lemniscate pull between solar and lunar orbs, and through the struggle gain that freedom which is his birthright, but which he is in danger of losing whenever he goes too strongly in the direction of either the Sun or the Moon. Whilst it is especially easy for us nowadays to see the manifestation or Ahrimanic forces in our arid materialistic cultures, in our stereotype, materially-based logical patterns of cerebration, it is perhaps more difficult to see the manifestation of Luciferic forces. Certainly it is easier for men to look on the Moon that it is for them to look on the Sun!

The traditional divinatory interpretation of the card is that the Sun presages great success, facility and clarity of expression, and good relationships – it is, of course, linked with general solar influences. In reverse it indicates failures, loss of valued goods and misunderstandings. It is certainly one of the strongest indications of creativity in the entire pack, and when the querent is female it may be symbolic of the male partner, especially when the question is involved with relationships.

The Sun is sometimes called Youth Eternal and (quite wrongly) Gemini.

202. 'The Moon' card 'The
203. Sun' Card are in sequence
to indicate that a lemniscate,
connected with spirituality is
required to complete the
circular motion of 'The Star'
with the circular design of
'The Judgement'.

204. 'The Triumph of Louis
the XIV' by Verner. The 'Sun'
King is shown with a
dazzling auriole contained
within a circular graphic
structure, rather like the Sun
of the Tarot cards. The
graphic structure is very
similar to that of both the
nineteenth and twentieth
Major Arcana.

205. An Italian version of
The Sun.

204

205

*206. An Italian version of
'The Judgement'.*

*207. 'The Judgement'
according to Waite. Observe
how Waite changes the central
mediating male figure into the
figure of a child, thereby
losing once more the whole
significance of the card.*

*208. 'The Judgement' with a
graphic analysis to show that
it is basically one of the
series of 'influence' cards.*

206

207

102

The twentieth card is meant to allegorize the idea of spiritual rebirth, no doubt arising from the emergence of the lemniscate in the previous two cards seen together in sequence (figure 209). The image depicts the angel of the Apocalypse sounding the last trump, with three naked human beings emerging from the tomb.

In some ways it is to be expected that the idea of spiritual rebirth should be presented in well-established biblical imagery, for the concept of man as dead or asleep, and therefore capable of being awakened, is one of the most recurrent themes in the Bible, a theme touched upon in the Moon card, and frequently symbolized in mediaeval art in terms of the tomb and resurrection (figure 189). Death, in the sense implied in this card, is found in the state of soul which has lowered its vibrational quality to such a point that it is completely submerged in earthly values symbolized by the tomb. This identification of sleep with materiality is emphasized by the angel holding the cross of Earth in his left hand, and by the colour of the hair of the naked people below, for blue suggests passivity.

The graphic structure of the card is extremely simple: the angel is contained within an aureoled circle, while the lower part of the card, which grips the three standing figures, is clearly another material square: the circle of spirit is raised above the square of materiality, and is attempting to influence it by 'quickening' it with life. To awaken, to find again the transcendental aim which is the main purpose of life, man needs grace from above, which is symbolized by the angel, or by a lifted circle, as in the raised host or crescent. The difference, in a spiritual sense, between men is the difference between those who await grace, in a state of preparation, and those who require to be jolted into a state of grace. It is to this latter group that the card applies, for the angel is required to make a trumpet noise sufficient to awaken them from their slumbers.

It is quite possible that the central human figure is meant to be a child flanked by its mother and father. This brings yet another association with the moon and sun of the previous two cards, for their conjunction gives rise to the conception of the child, who is then identified with the reborn spirit of man. Thus, we see that the happenings in the heavens (literally, in the upper parts of this and the last two cards) find a parallel on earth: the lonely savagery of the dogs below the moon, a common enough theme in mediaeval art (figure 208), represents alienation; the young couple under the beneficent light of the sun represent a relationship; in this third card a new

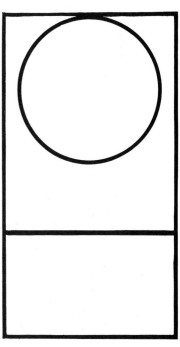

208

spirit is born, emerging naturally from the union of moon and sun. The isolated units in figure 209 show how the lunar and solar forces of the two previous cards are linked with the occult tradition with the Ahrimanic and Luciferic forces respectively, and how the dogs represent human beings reduced to mere animality, and the humans beneath the solar disc represent spiritualized beings. With this Judgement card we find a third element present – emerging, so to speak, from the tomb, along with the two elements of male and female. The female to the left of this third figure (who, significantly enough, has his back to us) represents the lunar Ahrimanic force, whilst the male to the right represents the solar Luciferic force. Standing between these two, at the midpoint of the lunar-solar lemniscate, we find the head of man. This is man as he should be – humanity who has succeeded in placing Ahriman and Lucifer in their rightful places: the Moon is on the right, the sun on the left, of Christ in crucifix pictures, but the Christ faces us, unlike this man of the Judgement card, so that the associations of left and right are still appropriate.

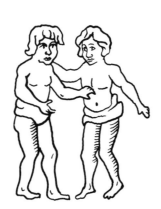

The fact that the man has not turned around to face us – to confront human beings as they are at present – symbolizes the truth that the conflict between Ahriman and Lucifer is continuing for humanity, and that there is every possibility that man may lose his freedom, if understanding and love do not grow within him sufficiently to make him aware of the need for struggle within the cosmic framework of his being. This is why the card truely does represent a Judgement – we are all being judged by our every action, by our every move, as we are still caught in the coils of this cosmic struggle between solar and lunar forces.

The presence of this card in a formal pattern promises a successful outcome to relationships or creative aspiration, provided the effects of lethargy are contended with. The card points to the fact that relationships must be worked at – they do not just happen as a result of two people meeting.

The traditional divinatory interpretation of the card is that the Judgement indicates regeneration, success in the face of difficulties, and legal judgements in one's favour. It is connected with solar and Mercurial influences. In reverse the card is supposed to indicate failure in enterprises, and the break-up of established ties.

The Judgement is sometimes called the Day of Wrath, which once again indicates just how far the divinatory traditions may stray from the path.

209

209. Schema to show the circular influence area of the last three cards operates on a series of progressively more spiritualized dualities.

210. Mediaeval manuscript. Note the influence circle of the triple Godhead the rays form from the wings of angles and a crescent moon upon which the Virgin and child are sitting. The whole design suggests that humanity is a product of the tension between celestial forces mediated by a celestial hierarchy and the Moon which stands at the lowest point of creation.

211. An Italian version of 'The Star'.

210

211

212. *The graphic structures of The World card and The Hanging Man card showing how the first links with the ascending force of Venus which is symbolized by the circle of spirit lifting up the cross of matter, whilst the latter links with Mars which was originally drawn as a cross of matter weighing down the circle of spirit.*

213. *The lectern support from a ninth century pulpit stand at Gropina, which incorporates the four symbols of the fixed signs of the zodiac, seen in Christian terms as the four apostles.*

214. *'The World'.*

215. *The derivation of the Venusian force of this card (see figure 212).*

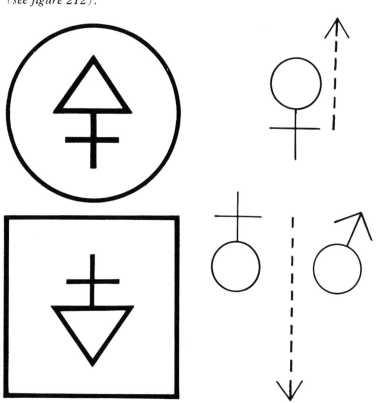

212

213

The twenty-first card of the Major Arcana is said by some commentators to be a summary of all the preceding cards, and it is consequently extremely difficult to ascribe a specific meaning to it all. The image is one of a naked woman inside a garland, with the four tetramorphs around her. This is *anima mundi*, the world soul.

It will be seen from the analysis at figure 214 that the posture of the woman is precisely the opposite of the one formed by the hanging man on the twelfth Arcanum – her feet are crossed (some commentators suggest that she is running, which misses the whole point of the card), and her hands are held out to form a triangle, suggesting the triad of spirit in glory over the cross of materiality. The reason for this interpretation is fairly obvious: the cross itself is the cross of materiality, connoting earth, weight and dead matter. The triangle suggests the trinity, and hence spirituality. In the Hanging Man of Scorpio the cross of matter is weighing down the triangle of spirit (figure 215), and the whole image is one of the world upside-down. In the World matter is subordinate to spirit – the triangle of spirit is dominating matter, and this is in the proper order of things: man is dignified in this position, and may emulate the gods by being creative. It is significant that the Hanging Man is a male figure, while the World is a female figure: the glyph for Venus, which in theory rules Taurus, and the glyph for Mars, which in traditional astrology ruled Scorpio, also reflect the philosophical implications of the two cards.

In Mars we see the vestigial cross weighing down spirit – thus creating a tension and violence which typifies the Martian urge to action. In Venus we see the cross being kept down by the circle of spirituality, echoing the idea of peace and rightness expressed in the twenty-first Tarot card.

The woman holds in her left hand a stick which recalls the magician's wand of the first Arcanum, and which has been interpreted as suggesting the dual polarity which lies at the base of all phenomena. We must recall that the single lines which make the material square express polarities – the diagram of the astrological cross at figure 42 shows the polarity which expresses the contrast between self and others, for example. The colour of the garland is probably meant to emphasize the idea of spiritual ascendancy, for the blue passivity of earth is in the lower part, the creative red is in the central part, and the gold of spirit is in the topmost part, paralleling in a curious way the concept of spirit discussed in this book.

The tetramorphs are symbols recurrent throughout Christian art: on one level they are obviously

Card 21 **The World**

THE WORLD

214

215

216

217

meant to symbolize the cosmic quaternity of Earth, Air, Fire and Water upon which all the elements of the created world are based, and their placing around the mandorla garland suggests (on iconological grounds) an attempt to associate the naked woman with the Pantokrator in other words to identify the human state with the god-like state.

The tetramorphs also represent the four fixed signs of the zodiac, as well as the Four Evangelists. The top left figure is the winged human of the Air sign Aquarius, usually associated with St. Matthew. Top right is the eagle, the old symbol for the Water sign Scorpio, usually associated with St John. Bottom left is the bull of the Earth sign Taurus, usually associated with St. Luke. Bottom right is the lion of the Fire sign Leo, usually associated with St. Mark.

On this level of understanding we see that the female *anima mundi* is placed within the zodiacal band as representative of the human condition in a state of spiritual grace. The full horror of those lopped tree trunks in the Hanging Man (figure 147) begins to emerge when the symbolism of the World card is grasped, for these were formed into the square of matter, imprisoning the hanging figure in a structure which was quite devoid of life. In the World card we see them transformed into leaves, arranged in a garlanded circle, framing a female figure. No more compelling state of spiritual change could be expressed with such economical graphic means. It could be, indeed, that the mandorla is composed of leaves in a subtle graphic reference to Christ's words on His way to Calvary: 'If they do this in the green tree, what will they do in the dry?' The single tree in Giotto's Arena Chapel *Lamentation* (figure 227) is reference to the same idea.

The card itself has been described as 'the Major Fortune', and it is certainly intended to be interpreted as the condition of balance and well-organized relationship between spirit and matter, for everything within the symbolism connotes a high quality of spirit.

The traditional divinatory interpretation of the World is that it indicates the successful achievement of an aim, and is linked with the Venusian and solar influences. In reverse the card is interpreted as indicating an obstacle to be overcome, as well as attachment to earthly things.

The World card is sometimes called Truth, the Cosmos, Mother Nature and Sophia.

218

LE MONDE

216. Details of the Gropina pulpit above the head of one of the twelve apostles (signs of the zodiac) we see head of Taurus the bull associated with St. Luke.

217. The lecturn at Gropina. In descending order is the eagle of Scorpio (St. John), the human face if Aquarius (St. Matthew) the lion of Leo (St. Mark).

218. An early French version of 'The World' card.

219. An Italian version of 'The World' card.

220. A Tetramorph incorporating in one figure the four fixed signs of the zodiac.

IL MONDO

219

220

221. An Italian version of 'The Fool'.

222. The titlepage of the first edition [1532] of Rabelais' 'Gargantua' – the graphic connexion with 'The Fool' is very striking, and is rich in allusion.

223. 'The Fool' the bag in the shoulder of the Fool contains the baubles of the first card, the embryonic four suites of the Minor Arcana. There is thus a link between this card and the first card of the Major set.

221

222

The unnumbered card of the Major Arcana consists of yet another statement of the condition in which man finds himself on this earth. It is an image of a fool wearing multicoloured clothing, with a lynx-like animal attacking his right buttock. On his right shoulder the fool carries a bag which, on the evidence of the first *atout*, we must assume contains the elementary forms of the Pentacle, Sword, Chalice and Sceptre. To the fool these treasures are merely so much of a burden, and their true value is unrecognized. The many colours of his dress suggest the multiplicity of the forces within him – the many different 'undisciplined squads of emotions' which react within him and drive him through life. He is not even looking where he is going, and the implication is that he is more interested in the audience – the person watching his passing (the querent) – than in his own path. Indeed later designers have made this point more obvious by placing a crocodile or an abyss before the path of the fool but, as usual, the original design is much more to the point. It is difficult to understand the symbolism of the lynx – or is it a dog? In the Italian pack it is certainly a dog, but for the Marseille pack we have only 'tradition' that it is a dog. It has been suggested that this animal is a symbol of remorse, but the idea is by no means easy to follow: the simplest interpretation must be that the creature represents the emotions driving the man along.

It is particularly significant that this is the only card without a unifying graphic structure, for this very omission is symbolic of the life of ordinary man, lacking structure and sense. It is hard to grasp that this structureless, rather sad card, which portrays a vagabond harassed by a fierce animal, wearing a fool's cap, and carrying a valuable treasure over his shoulder, is actually a portrait of oneself. Perhaps this is why it has no number: perhaps we should write our own name at the top.

When this card appears in a formal pattern it usually indicates two possibilities – that the querent should consider what he has (symbolically, look into the bag he carries), and that he should be prepared to set out in a new direction.

The traditional divinatory interpretation of the Fool is that it indicates passivity. It is not linked with any particular planetary influence. In reverse it is interpreted as indicating a blind impulse and lack of direction.

The Fool is sometimes called the Gypsy Vagabond, Adam-Kadmon, and even the Mate, which we must surely take as a corruption of the French *mat*.

223

THE FOOL

ROYNE · DESPEE

224

225

226

228

THE FOOL

224. The Queen of Swords from an early French pack.

225. The Ace of Clubs, which links with the baton, wands, and sticks of office which appear in the Major Arcana

226. Mediaeval image of death with his scythe.

227. 'Deposition' by Giotto. Arena Chapel, Padua.

228. 'The Fool'.

229. Waite's version of the Fool which totally loses the spirit of the original card.

227

THE FOOL .

229

230. *The Ace of Swords.*

231. *Two of Cups.*

232. *Two of Swords.*

233. *The Ace of Cups.*

234. *The Ace and Two of Deniers. The last six cards are examples of nineteenth Minor Arcana.*

230 232 233

The Minor Arcana

The Minor Arcana may be used, either alone or in combination with the Major set, for divination. However, beginners are strongly urged not to use the Minor set for answering questions or for divination, mainly because their use often requires the construction of complex formal patterns which confuse and bewilder, rather than clarify. At the same time, the Minor Arcana are symbols of a relatively fixed nature, and do not permit the latitude and sensitivity of reading which one associates with the Major pack. Several modern cartomancers of good repute are of the opinion that the Minor Arcana were never intended for divinatory purposes, any more than were ordinary playing cards – though, of course, cartomancers may often make use of both as springboards for intuitive judgements. There is a quality and grandeur about the Major pack which is entirely lacking in the Minor set and this alone should persuade against the use of the Minor pack for divination.

Popular cartomancy is based on the assumption that every pip card and every 'picture' card has a reasonably fixed meaning. Unfortunately my own researches, and the numerous conversations I have had with cartomancers, do not support this assumption. I have not been able to discern either rhyme or reason in the majority of popular meanings ascribed to the Minor set, or their derivative, the ordinary set of playing cards, and there appears to be no agreement between cartomancers as to what meaning should be attached to particular cards. The suggestion is that those cartomancers who use the Minor set, or ordinary playing cards, are working from direct intuitive response to the formal pattern, without any background knowledge of an underlying philosophy or occult system of interpretation.

This should not lead us to think that there is no such unifying theory behind the Minor Arcana, however, for there undoubtedly is, and this has been convincingly revealed by Papus. With this theory in mind, it is not necessary to learn the 'fixed' meanings of the 56 Minor cards: it is sufficient to master the elements of the theory underlying these meanings, and this will enable the student to work out the import of the cards as they appear in formal patterns.

The background to the explanation put forward by Papus is set out below: those readers who do not consider it necessary to follow the rationale behind the explanation are advised to turn to page 126, where the 'meanings' of the cards are listed, after a general explanation of the four suits or emblems.

Almost all religious and philosophical systems incorporate a theory of numbers which lend particu-

234

lar importance to the numbers three and seven. In Christian theology we are familiar with the number three in the Trinity of Father, Son and Holy Ghost; in the Indian *Sankhya* we find the three *Gunas*, modes of cosmic manifestation, *Tamas*, *Sattva* and *Rajas*; in astrology we see the relationship of Sun, Earth and Planets, which represent the active, passive and reconciling forces at work in the universe in alchemy we find the triadic process symbolized by the interaction of salt, sulphur and mercury. The comparison of the triadic theory could be extended almost indefinitely. In the Tarot the triadic force is also symbolized in terms of the cabbalistic name of God, *Yodhevauhe*, which must not be spoken. This is also, by extension, related to the number four. These ideas of the triadic nature of the world have been ably discussed by Rodney Collin in *The Theory of Celestial Influences*.

The number seven is the symbol of perfect order, comprising the unification of the ternary and quaternary in a complete cycle. The septagram, which is of such magical significance, is the graphic representation of the cyclical order.

It is said that although one might be able to understand the world in terms of either the triadic or septenary systems, it is not possible to see both these systems working at the same time. Because of this man in his ordinary state of consciousness cannot completely understand the nature of reality. He might be able to understand the world in terms of the operation of triads at one moment, and in terms of the operation of septenaries at another moment, but like a man focusing first on something in the foreground and then on something in the background, he can never see both working together, he can never focus at one and the same time on two different locations. The idea is, of course, that something working within the conditions of these two laws (i.e., the perceptual apparatus and the mind) cannot escape the conditions and apprehend the working of the Law.

The Tarot cards, as a philosophical system, enable one to study the workings of the ternary and septenary laws, and to see why it is not possible for the mind to encompass the working of both these laws in one. In fact, a little reflection will show that the two laws are actually a reflection of the nature of perception, and in themselves are the differentiating process by which reality is apprehended.

The law of three as presented in the Tarot is intrinsically bound up in the *Tetragrammaton*, the Hebrew name for God. The active, dynamic and creative force, the *Sattva* of the three *Gunas*, is the *Yod* of the Tetragrammaton. The passive, negative and material force, the *Tamas* of the *Gunas*, is the *He* of the Tetragrammaton. The resulting force which arises from the interaction of *Yod* on *He* is neutral, the harmonic *Rajas* of the *Gunas*, and forms the third letter of the name of God, the *Vau*. The fourth letter of the Tetragrammaton is a second *He*, regarded as a new unit which contains the forces of the first triad and yet marks a transition into a new sequence of manifestation.

This law, based on a subtle relationship between the numbers three and four, works on every plane. For example on a cosmic level we can see the influence of the creative sun (*Yod*) working on the passive earth (*He*) to produce formative life (*Vau*). These three forces, which are interdependent and inseparable, together are the manifestation of the cosmos, which is the second *He*. On the level of man, we see the family unit, the second *He*, as the interaction of man (*Yod*) on woman (*He*) to produce the child (*Vau*). The second *He* of man himself is a result of the workings of the triad of spirit (*Yod*), body (*He*) and soul, or sentiments (*Vau*).

The mysterious interplay of the law of three, the number four and the law of seven is expressed by the Square in the Triangle, which is a symbol of the Tarot. This pregnant symbol expresses the idea of the three containing the four, and vice versa. It can be produced quite literally by arranging the 22 Major Arcana to form an equilateral triangle, with seven cards to each side. In the centre of this triangle the unnumbered card (The Fool) is placed. Around the triangle is built a square from the 56 Minor Arcana, 14 to each side. The triangle is the graphic image of the Trinity, and represents the noumenal world. The square is the quaternity of the four elements from which the physical, phenomenal world is compounded. The single point at the centre of these forces is the soul of man, contained within the noumenal and phenomenal world (figure 237). The seven sides of the square and triangle diagram can be arranged in a different way, to represent the soul of man as standing within the framework of a square (figure 237).

One of the many interesting things about both these diagrams is that from where man is placed, in the midst of the interaction of phenomena and noumena, he can see only one part of the forces which make up the nature of reality. In the first diagram his perception is limited by the bounds of the triangle, and this symbolizes man perceiving the operation of the law in terms of triads, but not able to see the quaternity which surrounds it. In the second diagram he is limited to perceiving the four elements, the

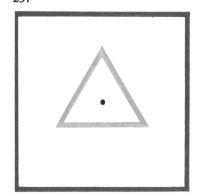

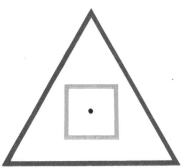

235. Detail of the Trinity from the picture at figure 210.

236. The name of Jehova in the clouds above macrocosmic man. According to one theory the sequence of the Minor Arcana depends entirely upon an interpretation of the name of God.

237. The Tarot structure represented in two philosophical machines.

238. Zodiacal man. Observe that the chalice is linked with the stomach area of Virgo.

238

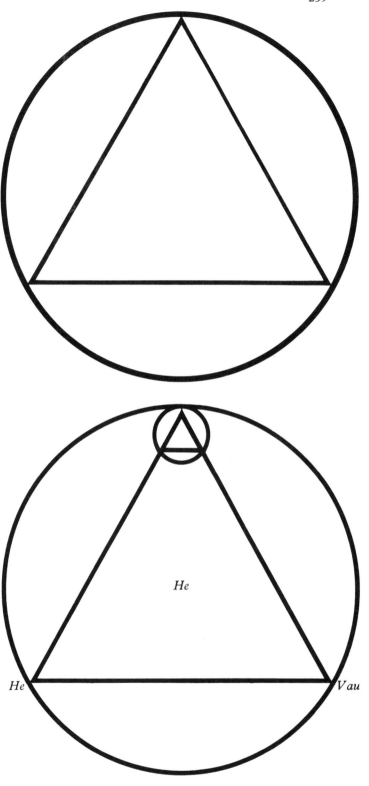

phenomenal world around him, and he cannot see the triadic forces outside the square. The diagrams therefore contain far-reaching speculations, representing the condition of man, limited by his own position and level of awareness to perceive only fragmentary aspects of the nature of reality. He sees the world of the senses (represented by the four elements) and is therefore enmeshed in the visible appearance of things, or he sees the world of noumenal forces (represented by the triangle) and is therefore enmeshed in spiritual values. In either case he is seeing only partial reality, for his vision is incomplete and unbalanced – the visionary and the gross materialist are equally removed from reality.

The diagrams show man in the midst of ternary and septenary forces, unable by virtue of his position to see the working of the forces together. It is clear that for man to perceive the conditions which do in fact surround him, and to become acquainted with the nature of reality, he must escape from his central position and, so to speak, rise above himself in order to examine the diagram from above. This action of rising above the level of ordinary perception has been equated by Ouspensky to the escape into the fourth dimension and the heightening of spiritual consciousness. We see that these diagrams are very impressive, though ancient, images of man in time.

The Tetragrammaton is written (236) *Yod-He-Vau-He* and although it has only three different characters and sounds, it consists of four letters. *Yodhevauhe* is the Ultimate: it is the Chinese equivalent of *T'ai Chi*, the 'ridge pole' which supports the 'ten thousand' things of manifest life. The *Yod* represents the active principle in the cycle of manifestation. It cannot express itself except as a part of the triadic sequence. The *He* represents the passive element which must complement the *Yod* in order to give rise to manifestation. In simple terms it can be thought of as woman in relation to man, the *anima* in relation to the *animus*. The interaction of *Yod* and *He* give rise to a third principle, which unites the active and the passive qualities. This is the *Vau*. Between them these letters or principles compose the triadic law of the Absolute.

These three forces interacting together produce a manifestation which in itself is a force belonging both to the triad, since it springs from the interaction, and to itself, since it is a force or principle in its own right. This is the second *He*. It contains the triad of the first, and it stands as a new principle, as a new *Yod*, in a position where a new triad can be formed. It marks a transition from one triad to another. The triadic action and interdepend-

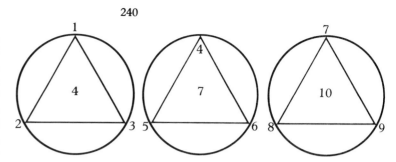

ency is most clearly expressed in diagram 240.

The second *He* is represented by the circle, which symbolizes the idea of the triadic interaction of *Yod*, *He* and *Vau* being contained within the second *He*. At the same time the second *He* must be thought of as commencing a new triadic arrangement (figure 240). The idea can be more simply expressed if we allocate numbers to the triadic sequence, as in diagram 240.

This simple theory of the name of God, *Yodhevauhe*, containing the nature of all manifestations may be applied to the Major and Minor Arcana of the Tarot in a very interesting way. With the Major Arcana we are able to follow the sequence by studying both the pictorial imagery in terms of the triad of forces, and the numerical significance of each card. The first triadic arrangement is merged with the second to give a septenary.

We have already seen that the second *He* stands as the *Yod* of a subsequent sequence, and that this may be presented diagramatically (figure 240).

The 4 acts both as a *He* and as a *Yod* – it contains the whole of the first triad and initiates a second triad. Clearly this relationship can be extended to ternaries, for they themselves are subject to the Law. We may, on this basis, take the first triad as corresponding to a *Yod*, a second ternary as corresponding to a *He*, and the interaction of these two producing a new force *Vau*, the whole triadic arrangement giving rise to a new *Yod*. This can best be presented in a diagram (figure 241) by inverting the second triadic triangle to symbolize its essential passivity. When these diagrams are combined, we arrive at the pregnant symbol of the Law shown in figure 241. This diagram contains the whole teaching implicit behind the arrangement of the Tarot cards. By a study of analogies we can see that 4 is the 1 considered as a negative principle, that 5 is a negative 2, and so on. Of course, the whole figure is actually the fourth *He*, which contains all the manifestations of the first septenary and yet marks a point of transition into a new triad which in itself forms the commencement of a new septenary (figure 239).

Just as the first two triads were combined to produce a septenary, so must the two septenaries be combined to form a new figure. The first septenary is a *He* or a negative force, and these should give rise to a new *Vau* which will be a neutral force. Each septenary contains one force which springs from and summarizes the preceding septenary, and yet properly initiates the septenary. There is an analogous arrangement between the forces within the corresponding positions – for example between the first *Yod* and the seventh *Yod*, and so on. The third

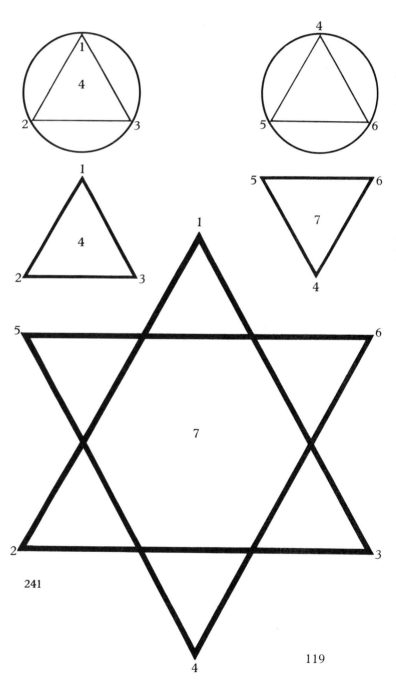

242. In numerical sequence of the Major Arcana related to the name Jehova.

243. The Lovers as the sixth completion of a cycle.

244. The Empress as a completion of the first cycle.

245. The Hanging Man as a completion of the second complete cycle.

246. 'The Moon' as completion of the third complete cycle.

247. The complete sequence of 22 Major Arcana.

septenary is symbolized as in figure 242.

The consideration of the third septenary brings us to the last three cards of the Major Arcana. These, in terms of the analogy we have followed so far, will between them contain all the forces of the previous septenaries, and yet represent a transition into another cycle of manifestation. These three cards (figure 242) are numbered 20, 21 and 0 (the unnumbered one), and mark the transition from the Major Arcana to the Minor Arcana. The analogies we have studied in this philosophical synopsis can be followed through to the Minor Arcana, and the correspondencies between the images and the numbered cards may be studied to some purpose.

It must be remembered that the analogies can be applied between the numerical positions, within the triadic sequences, though the first septenary is a *Yod*, the second is a *He* and the third a *Vau*. Thus, if we take Arcanum 6, the Lovers, we see that it is Arcanum 3, the Empress, considered negatively: they are both the *Vau* of the first septenary, yet Arcanum 6 is a positive *Yod* in relation to Arcanum 12, the Hanging Man. The meeting of these two Arcana results in the *Vau* of the eighteenth Arcanum, which is the Moon. This triadic relationship gives rise to the second *He*, the World, Arcanum 21. In the relationship we can study a psychological truth expressed by the hieroglyphics and which can be read on many levels: the question of decisions in its negative form (Arcanum 12) where the spiritual is weighed down by the material. The reconciling form, represented by the *Vau* of Arcanum 18 which stands for chaos, or the dead end of materiality. The moral of the triad is clearly that in the question of a spiritual decision, if no active conscious effort is made the end result can only be inner dissolution. On another level it is the image of mankind caught up in material consideration which can lead only to hell. This is a statement of the unconscious involuntary process in man and in nature. It indicates that only conscious creative effort can bring about spiritual progress. The transition marked by Arcanum 21, which in terms of the theory must contain the whole of the triad, is the move back into the world. In fact, as explained on page 107, the image of the naked woman in Arcanum 21 is exactly the opposite of the Hanging Man, Arcanum 12. The profound significance of the Tarot used in this way, as a philosophical machine, can only be understood when the significance of each card has been grasped to some extent.

The consideration of the philosophical basis of the Minor Arcana suggests that the four sets of cards will, when taken in a certain sequence, follow the

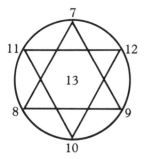

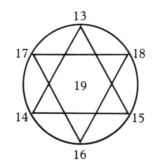

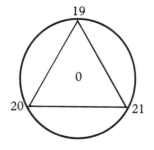

242

243

6

6

THE LOVERS

12

245

12

THE HANGING MAN

1

5   6

7

2   3

4

7

11   12

13

8   9

10

3

3

THE EMPRESS

18

18

THE MOON

13

17   18

19

14   15

16

19

0

20   21

244

246

247

248. One of the French set of Minor Arcana, 'The Chevalier' of Clubs.

249. The Jack of Swords from the same pack.

250. The Ace of Derniers.

251. An Italian Minor Arcana. The Queen of Chalices.

CHEVALIER DE BASTON

VARLET D'ESPEE

249

AR DE DENIERS

250

principles implicit in the name of God, *Yodhevauhe*. The Sceptre represents the *Yod*, the male active force; the Cup represents the *He*, the female passive force; the Sword represents the *Vau*, the union of these two forces, and the Pentacle represents the second *He*. Papus draws our attention to the analogy between these symbols and Christian doctrine: the Sceptre may be taken as the episcopal crosier, the Cup as the chalice, the Sword as the cross, and the Pentacle as the host, the physical manifestation of a transition from one world to another. The force of the creative spiral upon which the complex crosier head is based – and even the directional force of its simple crook form – indicates the depth of the analogy. The receptivity of the chalice, its image as a source, and its rich legend as the Grail is also very relevant. The hilt and blade of the sword are analogous to the vertical stroke of the cross, suggesting spiritual activity and energy descending from heaven; the cross-guard, analogous to the horizontal stroke of the cross, suggests passivity and balance. The ancient symbol for the meeting of the two prime forces of activity and passivity has found its most beautiful form in the image of the sword, exemplified by the high regard in which the Knights Templars held their weapons. The analogy between the host and the Pentacle, both philosophically and visually, is too apparent to need comment.

The Sceptre represents the magician's wand, which may be used for spiritual advancement or for material gain, and even the esoteric image hints at the power and force of this suit. In divination it is a symbol of creative endeavours, enterprises and physical labour: it is the manifestation of the beginning of undertakings.

The cup, as the association with the Chalice suggests, represents the domain of the emotions. Upright the cup contains blessings, but inverted it pours them away. In divination it is the symbol of love, the maternal wish for preservation, and teaching. It is the manifestation of the opposition aroused by commencing any undertaking – the natural force of passivity which must be resisted if progress is to be made. The force is not evil, however, for it is a necessary complement to the active order of things.

The Sword is the symbol of the meeting of these initiatory and opposing urges – the domain in which struggle takes place. This symbol of the meeting between the force of active and passive, expressed in the pre-Christian symbol of the cross, is confirmation of the idea that Christ did not bring peace, but the sword. In divination the sword is a symbol of the transforming powers, the struggle which can bring success or failure. It is sometimes suggested that the card stands for hatred, but I cannot find any justification for this belief – people may well hate struggle, and struggle may give rise to hatred, but in itself the reconciliation of opposing forces is merely a fundamental condition of life.

The Pentacle represents the result of the struggle, and contains the outcome of the attempt which was initiated, opposed and reconciled. It marks a new state of movement which must be initiatory. In divination it is a symbol of development, of money which in itself is a reward for effort, and it marks a new potential: it does not relate to money or goods received without effort, or to anything which does not result from the meeting of active and passive energy.

If we apply the above observations to the philosophical basis of the Tarot, we shall be in a position to see the divinatory meaning of each of the cards in the Minor Arcana. It must be noted that each of the four picture cards in the four suits represents a person. The King represents a man, the Queen represents a woman, the Knight represents a young man (or woman), and the Knave represents a child. The nature of these personages is traditionally determined by the suit to which it belongs, through the force of its symbol. This is why the divinatory meaning often links Sceptres and Cups with 'good' people, and Swords and Pentacles with 'bad' people, so that a King of Sceptres would be regarded as a 'good man'. In some ways this simple rule-of-thumb interpretation results from insufficient knowledge of the Tarot cards' nature: certainly the King will represent a man, but he must not be described in such a simple way – the card must be related to the suit in terms of its general meaning, and interpreted accordingly. Thus a King of Sceptres represents a man playing an important part in the initiatory force involved in the question which gave rise to the formal pattern of cards. A Queen of Swords, by the same reasoning, refers to a woman bringing opposition to the development of the matter under question, and it must not be forgotten that this opposition may well be necessary to the final working out of the issue; the formal order of the cards should indicate whether or not this is so.

The meaning of the number of the cards in each suit can be seen in diagram 251, in which C means Commencement, O means Opposition, and E means Equilibrium. The tenth card, as the theory might suggest, is the force containing all the elements in the triadic cycles which precede it in sequence; it also

251

REG. DI COPPE

marks a transition. The result is that it is an extremely difficult card to evaluate, and indeed Papus refers to it as a card which indicates uncertainty, as a card of undetermined meaning. Obviously the card is the meeting of all the forces, and contains all the possibilities of the particular suit under consideration; this must be borne in mind when it occurs in the formal pattern. It will indicate potential growth or possible loss, depending on its position within the formal pattern. When a card is dealt first in any kind of formal pattern it must be assumed that either there is no answer possible to the question or that the question is being wrongly put.

We can see from a brief glance at the diagram above why certain cards are associated with good and bad 'luck'. The seventh card is especially powerful, as it marks the final phase of equilibrium in an active way. The fourth card is the beginning of opposition, which is why the traditional systems generally hold it as being unlucky or bad. If we apply the triadic law of three cycles within one major cycle to each of the four suits we shall arrive at the following divinatory meanings for the numbered cards:

SCEPTRES

Ace

Relates to the commencement of an enterprise or undertaking which is relevant and important to the question asked.

Two

Indicates that there is an opposition to the commencement of the undertaking, and suggests that difficulties must be expected in the beginning – these difficulties may be overcome by persistence, but the original aim may have to be changed a little.

Three

The original aim of the undertaking will be preserved and will have a successful beginning. There is a tendency for the aim to need amending, though, if the next phase is to be successfully developed.

Four

A series of obstacles is being experienced (or will be experienced, depending on the nature of the question). Whether or not they will be strong enough to deflect the aim will depend very much on the formal pattern, but this is a strong card, for it represents opposition to all the three qualities of the first triad of commencement.

Five

Suggests that the opposition will itself lose force by natural involution or by the contradictory forces being deflected by outside interference. Although this is a card which indicates difficulty in the main enterprise, it is by no means as strong as the previous

252

124

252. *An early nineteenth century playing card, the Six of Diamonds.*

253. *Crowley's design for the Death card. Observe the intelligent introduction of Scorpionic imagery which links with the stagnation of Scorpio and at the same time hints at the regenerative nature of this card.*

253

card. It is sometimes read as 'opposition to the main opposition'.

Six

This card indicates that the undertaking will not be successful – whether this will be ultimately for the good or bad is a matter for careful interpretation.

Seven

The undertaking must succeed for the card represents the beginning of a co-ordination between the commencing impetus and the opposing forces.

Eight

Suggests that although the undertaking will succeed, the results will not be quite as expected – very probably the original aim has changed during the attempt to bring about its achievement.

Nine

Suggests both success and danger for, although the aim will come about, there will be a certain tendency towards stagnation. It is important that some new undertaking, in a quite different direction, be followed to avoid loss. The presence of a ten of any suit will indicate the direction which the new venture must take.

CUPS

Ace

Indicates the beginning of a new emotional entanglement, or a new subject of study, which is in some way relevant and important to the question.

Two

Suggests difficulty at the beginning: this need not (as Papus has suggested) spring from either the lovers or the emotional relationship. Its source (if this is important) must now be determined from consideration of the formal pattern, or by a separate question.

Three

The relationship is required by both parties, and it is important to their inner development.

Four

A serious obstacle to the emotional requirements being met – in love affairs this suggests quite definitely an outside interference. If this is a person, the picture card (not an *atout*) will indicate whom.

Five

Either some external influence removes or modifies an opposition to the development of the emotional elements involved in the question, or the force of the inception is sufficient to overcome the obstacle.

Six

The emotional factors do not reach a happy or successful conclusion, for the opposition has proved too strong. The outcome of this (and the cause) must be looked into before a prognosis is made.

Seven

Indicates that the emotional matter, be it some inner aim or a love affair, will achieve a fruition. In some traditional systems this card is taken to mean marriage.

Eight

Suggests that success in the emotional sphere will be only partial – the implication is that things change, and the two elements are not related in the right way.

Nine

There is a successful outcome of the emotional undertakings, but there is a new state of affairs demanding fresh directions. This is why the traditional systems often take this card to indicate motherhood.

SWORDS

Ace

The beginning of some undertaking involving considerable effort and struggle.

Two

There is a difficult beginning – the struggle must be very fiercely undertaken if the end is to be obtained.

Three

The force against which one is struggling will be overcome. Although the force is not entirely vanquished, the struggle is being made to some purpose.

Four

There is opposition entering from the outside, making the struggle even more difficult. This calls for a change of tactics – the idea is that things get more complicated.

Five

The forces are strengthened, and the card suggests that the undertaking will not succeed in its pure aim, in spite of all efforts. The querent is not strong enough, or sufficiently prepared, to win this struggle.

Six

The opposition is under control – a point of balance is reached, and the outcome of this balance will be interpreted from the formal pattern.

Seven

The struggle will be worthwhile, for the end will be achieved.

Eight

The card suggests only a partial success – something will certainly be gained, but something will be lost. The situation will be examined either within the formal pattern, or by a new question.

Nine

The struggle will last for some time, and the attitude to the struggle will probably determine what gains will be made. Struggle for its own sake must be undertaken as being one of the demands made by life.

PENTACLES
Ace
Beginning a new period of development, or financial gain, depending on the nature of the question. This card augurs well, whatever the background to the question. The gain may (with this card only) be unexpected.
Two
Initial setback to the development. This setback comes from outside, and is not expected.
Three
The development is to some purpose, and gains are made. This probably accounts for the fact that the card is often interpreted as meaning a small financial gain. Such a fixed meaning should not be adhered to, though it may mean that, within certain contexts.
Four
Opposition to all development will be experienced. Again, this card is usually interpreted to mean loss of money, and it can indeed indicate this. It is more exact, however, to interpret the card as meaning 'unexpected opposition'.
Five
The opposition to success is weakened by something, generally originating from outside the usual sphere of the questioner. This unexpectedly changes the force of the difficulties under which the questioner is attempting to make his new development.
Six
The card indicates that the opposition is sufficiently strong to balance the outward urge, and either ruin or considerable gain could result from this balance. The interpretation must be carefully made from the formal pattern.
Seven
The new period of development comes to fruition. In traditional cartomancy this card means 'a large fortune', but of course this interpretation is too fixed, and the meaning must be related to the background of the question.
Eight
Success in the development is only partial. The card suggests that the motives behind the wish for gain should be analysed.
Nine
The achievements, either spiritual or financial, will be considerable and lasting, which suggests that new ventures should be undertaken, otherwise a period of stagnation may set in.

254. A simple formal pattern for answering questions with the Major Arcana, the central card represents the querent the card on the left represents the force holding querent in the past whilst the card on the right shows the future tendency. The three cards here correspond to those drawn by Henry Cuffe (see page 10).

254

255. *An early nineteenth century version of The Sun.*

256. *A modern cartomancer using the Major and Minor Arcana in her own formal pattern.*

257. *The circular structure of the so-called Celtic formal pattern.*

255

256

Consulting The Tarot Cards

In response to a particular question the diviner will lay out the Tarot cards in a formal order, and then interpret the combination of symbols to which this formal order gives rise. Most psychologists will suggest that such a formal order is a kind of *autoscope*, a random collection of symbols into which the diviner projects his own particular sensitivity, giving an outlet for his subconscious which will enable him to answer the question, or in some way help the querent. Most occultists claim that the cards do not fall in a random pattern at all, but are arranged into a meaningful pattern by spirits. Whichever viewpoint one holds, it must be understood that the traditional advice concerning the construction of formal orders and methods of divination requires that the medium should prepare himself and the cards as though consulting the world of spirits. Thus, when we find the modern cartomancer Rakoczi (see bibliography, page 144), advising the seer to mentally conjure spirits prior to the consultation, we see that little has changed since the sixteenth century, when the occultist Agrippa wrote: 'But now because Lots are not directed always by mans minds, but also . . . by the help of other Spirits; nor is the minde of a Prophet always disposed to that excess of passion as we spoke of; hence amongst the Ancients, it was a Custome to premise before the casting of Lots, some sacred performances, in which they call upon divine intelligences and spirits for to direct the Lot aright.'

The nature of such 'sacred performances' will obviously depend entirely on the understanding of the diviner himself, but it is evident that one should not attempt cartomancy in a frivolous manner, or without some inner preparation. Most of the traditional rituals connected with such preparation are directed at quietening the body and sensitizing the spirit. A quiet room, an easy posture and a wide table are the only material requirements, but without a certain alterness of spirit, a state which is difficult to describe but which has a distinctive 'taste' about it, good divination will not be possible. Some cartomancers will occasionally do a reading for themselves, but it is extremely difficult to attain the kind of objectivity required: it is best always to have a medium, or someone familiar with the Tarot cards, to study the formal pattern on behalf of the querent, even when the querent himself knows how to interpret the cards.

With the exception of the time when the cards are actually being shuffled prior to the consultation, the medium alone is allowed to handle the cards, for they must be impregnated with his own 'mag-

257

netism'* if they are to work properly, and any adulteration of vibrations will undoubtedly interfere with his subconscious workings, or with his ability to contact spiritual levels through the agency of the cards. As a further protection it is sometimes recommended that a clean, silk-lined receptable must be used to contain the cards when not in use. Although nothing so formal as incense burning is required, as with the preparation for consulting spirits with the Chinese system of the *I Ching*, it is advisable to wash hands before handling the Tarot cards. An American writer advises the use of two packs for those who involve themselves with 'higher forms' of thought using the Tarot as a philosophical machine, as well as with ordinary divination; he reasons that the vibrational planes for the two methods are different, and to use only one pack may disturb the spirits.

The ritual of reading Tarot cards demands considerable spiritual effort on the part of the diviner, but certain demands are made also on the querent. He or she must be respectful and reasonably quiet within: sometimes this latter demand is difficult to meet, for the majority of people who genuinely need the services of a diviner are emotionally involved with the question they are phrasing, and find it difficult to establish a point of quiet within themselves. Because of this, it is sometimes useful for the diviner to talk with the querent before the consultation, and during the talk to permit his own quiet of mind to permeate the mind of the querent. A sense of inner quiet and strength of spirit is easily transferred to another person who is in a state of agitation. In certain cases it is useful prior to the actual construction of a formal order to discuss the framing of the question – most querents are only too strongly aware of the *feeling* of their question, but in their emotional confusion it is sometimes difficult for them to formulate in words precisely what the question is. An experienced cartomancer may help formulate the question, knowing full well that the Tarot will always give an answer by setting the problem within a much wider context than the querent himself is capable of grasping.

Some cartomancers will insist that if the cards suggest evil elements, or elements which might in some way upset the querent, one should either refuse to continue the reading, or attempt to soften the blow by amending the reading. The first solution, of withdrawing from the reading, is both irresponsible and dramatic, and should under no circumstances be indulged in. The second solution is no solution at all, for the whole point about serious divination is that

it is a shared experience, and must be shared to the full. If the cards present a dire picture of a difficult future, then they will also, by the very nature of their rich symbolism, indicate ways of action or lines of thought by which these difficulties may be best received and experienced by the querent. We all have to experience difficulties – this is partly what life is about – and any attempt to escape from them is at best a temporary expedient. Life is meant to be lived on many levels of experience, and very often the more unpleasant and restrictive the life, the more urgently will spiritual growth develop. It is, to my mind, one of the most excellent services which the divinatory sciences may provide, whether by means of the horoscope figure, by throwing coffee beans, or by the creation of a formal order of cards, to show a person in need of help *why* this help is necessary, and what spiritual growth may be expected from a distinct line of action. The most common question brought to clairvoyants is *what shall I do?* The good clairvoyant will not only say what the person should do, but will tell him *why he should do it.*

There is one other aspect of popular divination which must be mentioned. The astrologer William Lilly tells us with a strong moral tone about how shocked he was when his teacher, Evans, cast a horoscope for a lady, and then proceeded to interpret it in quite the wrong way: he predicted good things, when in truth the figures promised bad things. When later Lilly remonstrated with him, Evans confessed that he had done this because if he had predicted bad things – which is to say, if he had told the truth – then the woman would as like as not have refused to pay him. The moral is clear, and it is my firm conviction that money should not change hands for a reading. The Tarot is an important psychological technique, not to be used in a superficial manner: when the question is serious enough to warrant a reading, then the querent's feeling of gratitude for help received is payment in itself.

There are various schools of thought in cartomancy as to how the cards should be shuffled. It has been suggested, indeed, that only the medium should be allowed to touch the cards – this being a question of preserving 'magnetic influences'. On the other hand, certain other mediums insist that the querent should shuffle the cards, thus allowing his own vibrations to affect them and to produce a formal order independently of the medium. I myself follow the latter procedure, for it is essential that the querent should participate physically in the consultation, yet in such a way as to allow an objective

* There are very many words used for this 'personal vibrational quality' which permeates everything which we touch: 'magnetism' is perhaps as good a word as any.

appraisal of the meaning of the cards to be established.

In my own methods of consultation I make use of the Major Arcana only, and although one or two methods of consulting with the whole pack will be mentioned at a later point, the following rules may be adhered to in regard to shuffling. The cards are arranged in their natural numerical order, with the zero card, the Fool, in first place. The images are kept the right way up, numbers at the top, throughout the shuffling and reading: thus there is no reading for cards 'in reverse' as is sometimes found with other systems. I have adopted this stricture for many good reasons, but one must note that in any case the Major Arcana has a system of 'opposites' and 'reversals' built into its own graphic sequence – for example, the World is upside down in the Hanging Man, as the analysis of the graphic structure at page 70 demonstrates. There is no need to obtain literal reversals of cards.

The pack is placed on the table in front of the querent, who is asked to shuffle the cards thoroughly, and then cut them. When the shuffled cards have been returned to the table, the querent is asked to form the question, quietly to himself, as though to feel the force of his question within, and whilst doing this to shuffle the cards and cut them as before. When this had been done, and the cards are once more face down on the table, the querent is asked to frame the question as simply as possible, and aloud, in order that the diviner himself may hear it. If for any reason the diviner considers the question frivolous or unanswerable, he should close the consultation. Once more the cards are shuffled, cut and returned to the table. This is the last contact that the querent has with the cards. At no point during the shuffling should the querent see the images themselves. During this three-fold shuffling ritual, the diviner is attempting to relax his body, and to gather his attention so as to empathise with the querent at the time when the question is posed. It is important that a spiritual equilibrium and a sense of objectivity be established before any attempt is made to interpret the cards.

The diviner should take up the cards and deal them out very slowly, in the pattern and order indicated below. As each card is revealed, the diviner must relate its significance to the place it occupies. We observe that in this particular formal order there are two different structures, one of which resembles a cross, the other of which is a straight line of cards. In fact, these two different groups are related horizontally, card 4 with card 7, card 3 with card 9,

258. The completed Celtic formal pattern. The numerical sequence for laying out the Celtic formal pattern.

259. An example of the first three cards in the Celtic formal pattern.

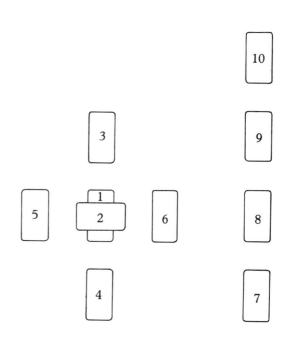

and so on, leaving the tenth card standing above the rest, and aloof. This card is not really involved in the 'action', for it symbolizes what will be the final influence, the result and outcome of the matter raised by the querent in the formulated question. It is likely that this Celtic system incorporates one group of six cards and one group of four for philosophical reasons: add together the digits from 1 to 6 and the result is 21, which is the number of figured cards in the Major Arcana. The group of six cards relates to the position of the querent in regard to the question, and they are all involved with questions of the self in relation to spirit and matter (the trinity of spirit enmeshed in the trinity of materiality). The line of four cards is, as we have noted, really three cards (half of six), with one card standing aloof, and this trinity stands for spirit liberated from matter. This group of three deals with the spiritual side of the question, which is why they are interpreted upwards, from bottom to top, ascending to the spirit, and towards the tenth card which summarizes the entire figure. The three, as half of six, deal with only one half of the querent's nature, with his spirit; the tenth card summarizes this spiritual ascent. The diagram below sets out the actual 'movement' of the eyes in the study of the sequence of this formal pattern.

The cards in this formal pattern have a rich set of associations, many of which will become clear only through practice. The first card represents the querent in relation to the question itself. The second card represents the obstacle which is giving rise to the problem involving the question. The third card symbolizes the conscious aim of the querent relative to the question. The fourth card represents the subconscious aim of the querent relative to the question. The fifth card represents the querent himself, whilst the sixth card represents the field of relationships with others, relevant to the question, however indirectly. The seventh card symbolizes the attitude which the querent holds to himself, for this is of great importance in determining the outcome of the question. The eighth card symbolizes his environment, the spiritual force of the situation involved with the question. The ninth card symbolizes the hopes and fears of the querent, thus summarizing the previous two cards. The important tenth card symbolizes the outcome, a nodal point where all the influences within the two united structures join together to form a new influence in the figure.

It will be helpful at this stage to examine the relevance of the formal pattern in regard to actual interpretation, in order that one may grasp the spirit in which interpretation must be conducted. As we do this, it will become evident that the formal pattern is of paramount importance in interpretation, for the places in which the cards are distributed within the formal pattern influence profoundly the symbolism of their images, and thus qualify the interpretation which must be applied to them. Their significances change in much the same way as the significance of the planets of astrology change, depending upon the area or degree of the zodiac in which they are located. Just as the Sun in Taurus manifests in a very different way from, say, Sun in Leo, so would the Juggler express a different quality of action in say a first position within the formal pattern, than it would in the eighth position. From this it will be realized that the aim of any good medium or cartomancer will be to see the formal pattern as a whole, and to allow his quietened intuition to unite with his profound knowledge of the associations and forces of the individual cards, and from this to allow the interpretation to arise almost spontaneously.

Before we do examine the formal pattern and relate it to card interpretation, we must observe that for the purposes of explanation it will be necessary from time to time to examine the symbolism of individual cards in isolated card placings: whilst this is necessary, towards the end of explaining the Tarot, we should realize that it does tend to give a wrong impression of real cartomancy. In genuine card interpretation one is involved with attempting to catch the 'whole' situation, to evaluating the issues which arise from the dynamic interplay of cards within the formal structure. This is possible only after considerable experience, and although here we must examine the individual card placings within the formal pattern as if they stand in isolation, the beginner should not lose sight of the fact that this does give the impression that cartomancy is a matter of interpreting individual cards and adding together their significances, as though they were some kind of digits. Real divination is involved with a kind of reverse perception, for one has to see the whole, and work from the whole to the particular, yet one must at the same time be aware that the whole is composed of particulars. The precise taste of this 'somersault' will be experienced by anyone who attempts seriously to use the Tarot for even a short time.

Something of the depth of the Celtic formal pattern may be realized if we look at it in a slightly different way from normal, observing that the dynamic interplay of forces consists essentially of dualities and triads. The first two cards dealt represent the querent in relation to the problem set by the question: sometimes this problem is apparent from the question, sometimes it becomes apparent through the analysis, but at all events, this second card laid across the first certainly represents the obstacle with which, consciously or not, the querent is faced. This pair of cards forms the 'cross' he has to bear. The third card laid above the cross symbolizes the aim of the individual, in the dual sense of materiality and spirituality. It represents the tenth house cusp of the horoscope, and is therefore linked with status, control, aspirations, and all matters concerned with the hopes and wishes of the querent in regard to the question. It is, however, much more involved with the material world than the ninth card, which represents spiritual hopes, wishes and fears. The first group of these three cards is of very great importance in regard to setting the general theme of the response: they constitute the 'theme triad' of the question, and between them they represent the basic forces which have given rise to the question (figure 259). If one were to find this triad disposed as in figure 260 for example, with the Wheel of Fortune crossed by the Empress and the Justice above them, one would see immediately how the graphic interpretation of the symbols results in a clear theme. This triad was the beginning of a formal pattern obtained in response to a question from a young girl who was thinking of abandoning her University career: her question was, "what shall I do?"

The querent finds herself, in terms of the reading, caught in the eternal circle of the wheel, constantly revolving, constantly on the periphery of life, and with no centre to her being. The diagram at figure 109 shows how the large circle of the Empress card, so evocative of materiality, indicates the clutching at materiality, for the hands within the circle grasp at emblems of power (figure 260), and so we must presume that the problem represented by this circle resting directly over the wheel circle must be involved with materiality. It is the interpretation of the wheel and the circle which lend a new interpretative value to these two cards when so juxtaposed. The small figure seated above the Wheel of Fortune is seen above the 'cross' card, and is in any case isolated from the rotation of the wheel: in this formal pattern it is curiously emphasized because Justice is a larger version of this figure, and is above the crossed pair, suggesting that the aspiration of the querent is involved with isolating herself from the

259

133

material *maya*, the illusory, transitory world, in order to look down upon herself, so to speak; in order to clarify her position by becoming uninvolved. Justice in this series has wings, symbolic of spiritual power, and we gain the impression from the triad that the answer to the question will be expressed in terms of the hope that its querent will be able to 'fly', that is, rise above the problem. The presence of the Justice above the crossed cards is usually an indication of a need to deliberate carefully, but in this particular context is an indication that there is a need to deliberate carefully about one's relationship to materiality. The advice offered by the remaining cards confirmed this theme, and the querent was advised to ask the University authorities to allow her a year's leave of absence until she found if she really wanted to continue with her present course.

From the hint that the third card position is connected with the tenth house of astrology, those with a knowledge of astrology will guess that the four cards distributed around the dual cross mark out the angles of the horoscope. This is true, and the following notes on the four important angles will serve to enrich the significance of the nodal points represented by the third, fourth, fifth and sixth card placings. The first house is called the Ascendant (represented by card placing number 5) and is the strongest single point in a horoscope, representing the accumulated forces of the personality. It is the house of selfhood. Opposite to this house is the Descendant (card 6) which represents the area of relationships, a house which is often termed in astrology 'The House of Marriage', though it relates more to the idea of general relationships in the sense that the selfhood of the Ascendant wishes to emerge in union with another human being, and lose the isolation of selfhood. These two houses are of profound importance in cartomancy when studying relationship problems involved with the question. For example, in a formal pattern which gives the Sun as the fifth card, and the Popess as the sixth card, one may presume difficulties in relationships. These may be read in terms of the radiating force of the Sun in the Ascendant creating too much self-love, a selfish strain (though sometimes it may also indicate a preoccupation with some creative endeavour), which drives the partner away: the Popess in the Descendant house is looking away from the book on her knee, which in cartomancy is taken as an indication of lack of interest. The head of the Popess is level with the 'head' of the Sun, and she is looking at the male symbol, rather than at her book – this is itself significant when the querent is female.

Perhaps more important is the two areas of the blue mantle in the material square over the knees of the Popess, for they are echoed in the structure of the twins, below the Sun. Blue in the Tarot cards always indicates passivity, while the twins are filled with Mercurial animation. One might presume from this, depending of course on the force of the triad which separates the two cards, that the problem arises because of too much passivity in the female, and too much activity in the male: that, for example, they lead different life tempos. Were these cards reversed, with the Popess on the Ascendant, then the female would be seen as showing great interest in the male, though the male would appear to be more interested in the couple below him – indicative of jealously in the female querent, of duplicity in love matters in the male querent. It is of course, extremely difficult to generalize about the nature of cards in isolation, and it is done here only to indicate the general principles of interpretation using the Celtic method.

Just as the fifth and sixth cards find a correspondence with the Ascendant-Descendant line, which actually marks day from night in a horoscope (figure 260), the third and fourth cards correspond with the M.C. and the I.C. of the horoscope. The M.C. marks the highest point in the sky which the sun reaches, and the abbreviation stands for *medium coeli*, middle of the heavens: the point thus symbolizes perfectly the aspirations of the querent, the point to which he strives quite openly, 'in the light of the sun'. The I.C. marks the lowest point which the sun reaches in its apparent movement around the earth, and the abbreviation stands for *immum coeli*, the bottom of the heavens: the point symbolizes the 'hidden', subconscious drives of the querent, the forces which are obscured by the darkness of night, yet which drive the querent onwards, The card in this fourth place is often very important when the question is involved with an illness or a mental state: again, it sometimes hints at an influence or factor within the context of the question which is not recognized by the querent. One observes the same kind of relationship between these two card placings as with cards 5 and 6: they express polarities of relationships, the topmost card representing a liberating influence for those energies contained in card 4, just as card 6 represents a liberation from the selfhood of card 5.

When we move to card 7 in the interpretation of the formal pattern we leave behind the complex interaction created by the cross, the pulls and attractions which symbolize the querent's problem, and we move into the simple structure of the ascending row of cards which between them reveal the outcome. This row stands partly removed from the complex figure, though, as we have noted, the first three cards do reflect the six cards to the left. These placings have a directness about their symbolism which is in itself represented by the fact that the dealing and reading (figure 263) becomes simple, and disengages itself from the spiral movement of the first six cards. If we can grasp the quality of this freedom, we understand the real significance of this ascending line within the formal structure. The seventh card 'reflects', as it were, the fourth card, and therefore represents the spiritual outcome of the involvements considered through the fourth card: it sets the tone for the quality of spiritual energies which ascend above it, and which find liberation in the tenth card. The eighth card placing represents the spiritual summary of the central cross as well as the fifth and sixth card placings, and so we see that when it is called the card of 'environment', this expresses only part of the function it represents. In a sense the eighth card is the spiritual summary of the most important elements in the question, acting as a kind of lens which intensifies the force of first, second, fifth and sixth cards.

One has to consider the ninth card placing in two ways: first, it is the spiritual echo of the third card, and is therefore involved with the spiritualized aim which has emerged from the question; and secondly it must be considered as standing in between the eighth card and the tenth, acting as a barrier between the two. The card represents the fears of the querent, as well as his hopes, in regard to the spiritual outcome of the question. Ideally one would require there to be no ninth card, so that the energies of the eighth place, which summarize the question so precisely, could be transferred directly into the tenth place, and thus become directly the 'solution', the final spiritualized outcome of the question or action which was initiated in the first six cards. But the ninth card stands there as a kind of sentinel, as a tester of the querent: fundamentally this card placing is involved with the question of love in its most spiritualized sense. The opposite emotion to love is fear, and fear is an isolationist force for it tends to cut off the querent from the object he strives for. Thus, if we find a strong indication of tension or fear (such as the Hermit or the Hanging Man) in this place, we may presume that there will not be an easy transition from the eighth to the tenth card, for something within the querent is not

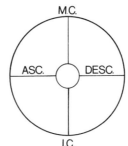

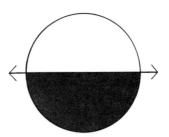

260. *The four angles of the horoscope and the light and dark division of the horoscope.*

261. *The relationship between the four angles of the horoscope and the third, fourth, sixth and fifth cards of the Celtic formal pattern.*

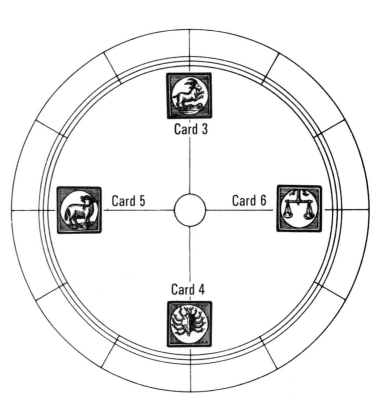

261

135

relaxed enough (sometimes in a physical sense, sometimes in a spiritual sense) to permit the transition.

The tenth card symbolizes the outcome of the question, takes one beyond the actual confines of the question, and refers really to the end product of the factors involved within the nine other cards. This is why it stands isolated from the rest of the set. In some cases it points to the outcome, if the line of action advocated by the cards is not followed. One must determine which of these is most important from the structure of the cards in the last line of four. For example, the set of four cards at figure 263 illustrate the right hand group obtained in response to a question put by a middle-aged woman concerning the man in her life. Her experience in the past had led her to fear male contact, through a sense of being let down. The reading proceeded along the following lines.

You are at the moment the Hermit, lonely and alone, peering into the darkness, feeling your way with the stick which we saw in the earlier cards. (This was the World card in third place.) You observe that the figure is wearing a red cape, roughly forming a square – this suggests activity in the material sphere. The man is wearing a blue hat, which suggests passivity in the intellectual sphere, indicating that the problem is one of attitude: you are alone, and may remain alone because your attitude is wrong. It is necessary for the red cape to become blue, and for the blue hat to become red, so that you will have an entirely different relationship to yourself and to your body: your perceptions (symbolized by the head) must become more alert, more discriminative. Examine the upper part of the two cards above this Hermit *atout*, and you will see what possibilities are open to you, if you can adopt a new attitude: the head becomes first a star, which is an active source of light, and which is the perceptive act guiding one onward, away from the passive blue of the head. Above this, and in the same position, is an even more intense form of the star, as seen from the solar system, the male symbol of the Sun, radiating out energy and force. We need scarcely examine the symbolism of the change from the stick and the lamp (which is the human light, transformed into a stellar light, later transmuted into a solar light), through the two goblets, which some say represent the sun and the moon, with all the associations of the male and female attached to these luminaries, to the open assertion of a human relationship which we study in the two figures standing below the sun. In these first three cards of

the second order, an order which refers specifically to the future, we see two sets of symbols joining together in indicating that there will be growth towards relationship with a male, a double growth symbolized in the following way:

Card The Sun.
Top Half Radiating sun, symbol of creative male.
Two Symbols Two human beings linked physically in relationship, and held together spiritually by sun.
Card The Star.
Top Half Sirius, symbol of need to move to a distance, and become oneself a guide.
Two Symbols Two goblets, pouring water. The woman is alone and naked but there is a guide above. The water fructifies the dry earth quality which is characteristic of the card below.
Card Hermit.
Top Half Head, wearing blue as symbol of passive attitude. The head looks only into the past.
Two Symbols The light and the stick with which he feels his way along. The light of human manufacture will be transformed into the star, and then the Sun. The stick, with all its sexual associations, must be transformed into a goblet, which will contain spiritual force, and then into the deeper 'goblet of spiritual force', the human being.

We might find it curious that, with all this promise of a coming relationship leading up to the ninth place, the tenth card should appear to roundly contradict the spiritual ascent by interposing a demonic force. The card must be understood as pointing to the outcome, if the demands made in the Hermit card at the bottom of the ascent are not met. The Hermit card requires a change of attitude: the querent must turn round, and stop looking only into the past (see page 59); she must become more active mentally, and change her attitude, or perception of the world (put on a new cap, so to speak); she must drop the weighty bag she is carrying, in which, occultists affirm, are dead memories. If she succeeds in reorientating herself, then it will be possible to establish a new and vivifying relationship with a man, as the promise of the Sun card holds. If she does not, then the forces of the devil will hold sway: she will become more isolated, more and more enmeshed in darkness.

It is necessary to study the true force of the tenth card by relating it to the preceeding three, as is evident from the above example. It stands serene, both as promise and threat. If it openly threatens, then one must look for the demand for change which the rest of the pack must offer. No divinatory system will say *this* will happen, though most divinatory systems will say *this will inevitably follow on this*, and will usually offer a way to avoid an unwanted experience. If we reflect upon this isolated tenth card we will begin to understand something about the occultist view of life: occultists tend not to interpret the flux of life in terms of such animistic concepts as 'beginnings' and 'endings' but recognize an interconnexion between things which make every 'ending' a new beginning. Because of this we must consider the tenth card as being both initiatory as well as completing. In a sense, besides marking the outcome, besides standing outside the periphery of forces set up by the other cards, it in theory at least* stands as the beginning of a new cycle, waiting to be crossed by another card, to initiate the spiral of a new dynamic interplay. The particular nature of this card placing may be understood only when the occult view of flux is grasped. If we return to our graphic analysis of the formal structure, we may see that the simplicity of the movement upwards, with its attendant clarification and spirituality, lends only to another involvement in complex spiral formations.

The Celtic formal pattern therefore reflects the nature of life (physical life, as represented by the combining of the two triads), punctuated by involvement with spirit (the three lower cards of the right hand range). Occults are aware of this pulsation on every level, from waking and sleeping, to living and dying.

My experience of the Tarot cards leads me to regard the 'Celtic' method as the most satisfactory, but there are several different forms of constructing a formal pattern which are worth looking at, if only to see how diversely the cards may be applied to human problems. One or two methods have become hallowed by traditional usage, but individual cartomancers usually develop their own formal pattern in much the same way as they develop their own personal 'style' of interpretation. There are methods as complicated as the one called *The Tree of Life of the Questor*, which involves all 78 cards in a triple reading of past, present and future; methods which link directly with astrological patterns and require considerable astrological knowledge for correct evaluation, such as the one recommended by Hades, using 36 cards in twelve groups of three, within the circle of the horoscope; and methods as simple as the one advocated by Papus, which needs only four Minor Arcana and seven Major Arcana for a simple reading.

---

* *I am here dealing with philosophical speculations: in the actual reading this card does 'terminate' the action of the formal pattern. To understand its force aright, however, we must regard it as commencing a new movement in life. This card is a kind of seed thrown from the floriating plant of the matured formal pattern. The whole philosophical background to divination on this level is in any case linked with the law of 'karma'.*

262

262. An example of the linear summary of the Celtic formal pattern.

263. The spiral movement of the first six cards in a Celtic pattern is given a single strong upward linear movement as a final summary of the outcome of the forces contained within the cards.

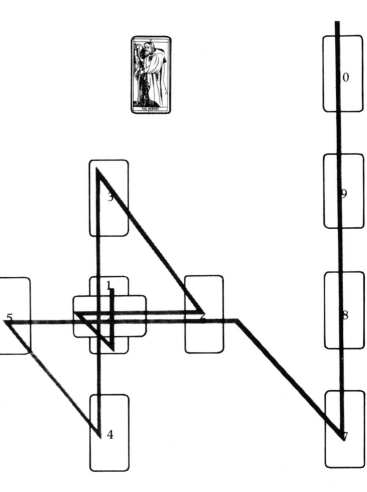

263

264. The Temperance card reproduced by 'Aliette', one of the most influential and at the same time one of the most unreliable of all commentators on the Tarot.

265. A Cabbalistic diagram of the macrocosm, containing various graphic devices found within the structure of the Major Arcana.

266. The mediaeval image of Virgo, which may be compared with the Temperance card.

267. A French version of The Emperor card.

264

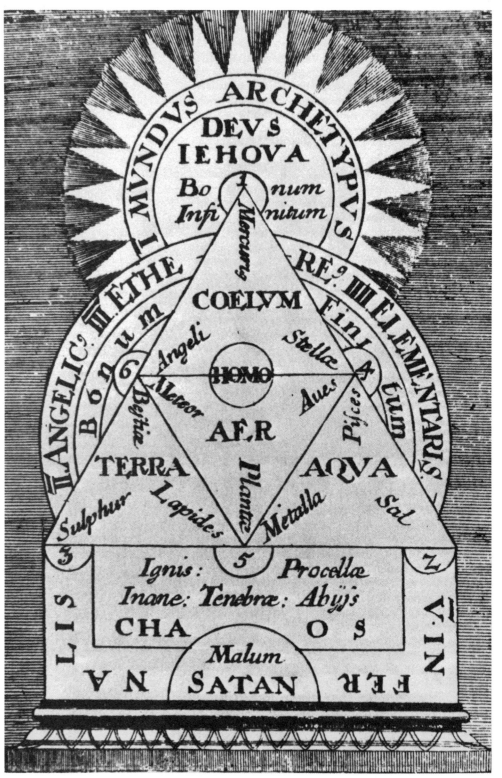

265

The Historical Background to The Tarot

Any history of the Tarot cards can be little other than an extended commentary on human credulity, duplicity, inventiveness, ignorance and superstition. The Tarot cards were certainly in use at the beginning of the sixteenth century, and this is all we truly know about their origin. Perhaps they were used at that time for divination, but we are not sure even of this.

It is reflective of the general confusion and ignorance of the majority of writers on the Tarot that the pack should have been variously described as being of Egyptian, Bohemian, French, Oriental and even Celtic origin. In the rare cases when a commentator is intelligent enough to disclaim such origins, as well as dispute the general hoary antiquity attached to the cards by irresponsible writers, the tendency is still for him to rapsodize about their scope and intention in a manner which does more to obscure than to clarify. A. E. Waite, having disposed of many of the more ridiculous superstitions concerning the Tarot, thus clearing the ground for the promulgation of his own fantastic superstitions, writes in a typical manner, 'The Tarot is, of course, allegorical – that is to say, it is symbolism – but allegory and symbol are catholic – of all countries, nations and times; they are not more Egyptian than Mexican; they are of Europe and Cathay, of Tibet beyond the Himalayas and of the London gutters.' All this is so much rubbish and we shall return to such spurious ideas at a later point. However if only to inject a certain degree of clarity into the confusion, we must observe that the so-called Marseille pack, which must be regarded as the only genuine of the surviving packs in general circulation, appears to have been based on Italian originals, and has a late mediaeval flavour, both in design and iconography.

The underlying structures of these cards are in essence mediaeval rather than neo-platonic. They express simple structural symbolism of a style that was familiar to monastic scriptoria, rather than the more sophisticated manner of Renaissance designers.* The graphic structures and the general quality of design point to a fifteenth-century origin, but much of the symbolism is of a much earlier date, and combining pagan and Christian symbolism in a manner evocative of the Romanesque. Numerous examples may be cited of such literary and iconographic throwbacks – for example, the Fool may be traced back to such images as the Wandering Jew, the cupid in the Lovers performs the same function as in Botticelli's *Primavera* (figure 99), though it is a symbol rooted in a classical past, and we must observe that the dress and hair-

Something of the force of the change in such graphic structures, which were mainly a result of the dissemination of the ideas of Paccioli and Alberti may be traced in the excellent book on such structures by Charles Bouleau.

267

139

style of the man below this cupid is clearly Italianate. Again, the curious symbolism of the Juggler in his fylfot gesture with rod and circle, finds a curious parallel in the *Mocking of Christ* fresco in San Marco.

If such evocations are not sufficient to support the contention of an Italian and mediaeval origin, we must observe that the falling figures in the House of God are found in a manuscript version of mediaeval Italian origin, as well as in a statuary detail at Reims Cathedral (figure 176). Again, the polarity motif underlying the contrary pull of the red and blue horses in the Chariot is found in several mediaeval manuscripts, a particularly striking example of which is preserved in the Bodleian Library, Oxford (figure 98).

The earliest sets of cards linked with the Tarot are of Italian origin, and were either designed or copied in the late fifteenth century, though the purpose of these cards is unknown, and there is no evidence that they were used for divination. In any case, though certain of these early packs do contain several of the Major Arcana in the form we know them today, many of the cards have no direct link with the modern Tarot, as those from the Andrea Mantegna pack demonstrate.

The cards which must be considered as being the best currently available are those known as the Marseille pack, which quite clearly maintain certain iconographical details and symbols of a very early period. The cards were printed as late as 1761 by Nicholas Conver in Paris, though they appear to have been based on earlier models produced by such printers as Arnoud (1748) and Dodal, whose designs were executed in the first decade of the eighteenth century. The survival of such packs into modern times accounts for the fact that the 'Italian and mediaeval' designs bear French names. Again, it is reflective of the ignorance of so many soi-disant authorities that the French nomenclature for the cards has resulted in one tradition that they were of French origin: the cards are no more French than they are Egyptian or Indian! It is evident that these cards were 'not created by spontaneous combustion', as Jean-Marie Lhote puts it, 'they had antecedents and parallels which are at once Pagan and Christian.'

Looking into the history of the cards, one cannot but be surprised that so many irrelevant and chimerical ideas have been attached to these remarkable images. There are several reasons for this, perhaps the most important being that the cards are quite clearly of an esoteric origin, and do in fact conceal a hidden symbolic language, which many commentators have consciously or subconsciously sensed and

have attempted to reveal in their own personal way, usually to the detriment of the cards themselves. Another reason for the existence of so many chimerical ideas is connected with the kind of person, the quality of being, of the majority of people who have been attracted to the Tarot cards in the past – those self-styled adepts who used the cards for divinatory purposes, or merely for the sake of making money, generally knew little about symbolism, and nothing at all about history, with the result that the attempt to trace the history of ideas behind the Tarot pack inevitably ended up as a sad commentary on chicanery, self-deception and superstition.

Only too frequently the prejudices of a particular time or of a particular individual have resulted in hypotheses concerning the cards which have been accepted by the credulous as proven facts, however much conflict there is between such 'facts' and the evidence of the cards themselves. For example, the understandable excitement concerning Egyptian hieroglyphics prior to the discovery of the Rosetta stone, led Court de Gebelin to announce that the cards were of Egyptian origin, and that indeed the word Tarot meant 'Royal Way', supposedly derived from *Tar* (Road) and *Ro* (Royal). The theory could have been demolished by anyone who cared to examine the Christian and pagan symbolism contained within the cards, yet the idea of an Egyptian origin has persisted, to such a point that many people to this day refer to the Tarot as the 'Book of Thoth'.

A further complication is that there are actually many different Tarot packs. Within the body of the main tradition of packs, we do find various slight variations in actual details of symbolism: for example, the Fool of the Charles VI set is a giant; in the Visconti pack the Pope does not have the kneeling figures in front of him. Such differences are on the whole unimportant and usually may be ignored. However, there is a much more serious side to the question of variation, and this springs from the fact that almost every 'adept' or 'authority' on the cards has made an attempt to redesign, restore or clarify the images, almost always with disastrous results. The end product is a wide variety of different 'Tarot' packs of different and usually indifferent designs, many containing the personal symbolism and psychological complexes of their designers. For example, A. E. Waite, who perhaps should have known better, had a new set 'drawn and coloured by Miss Pamela Colman Smith', thus lending his important name to a set of cards which are now used by very many cartomancers, but which merely succeed in obliterating virtually all the esoteric content of the original Tarot packs. Waite has a great deal to answer for,* not only because of the dreadful quality of his own cards, but also because of the way he has prevented people from grasping the real import of the Tarot by completely missing it out from his own set. It will be evident to anyone who follows the main themes of this present book that the Waite pack may in no way be considered a serious Tarot set, and indeed suffers from ignoring the conventional archaisms and colportage of the earlier packs to which Waite objects, and which in fact he was quite incapable of understanding.

The tendency is to criticise Waite because of the profound influence he has had on the conception of the modern Tarot, and because it is a tragedy that his own cards are so frequently taken to be genuine Tarot. However, Waite is not the only person who has invented his own set of cards, and passed them off with high-handed promise of esoteric meaning: a striking example of graphic and symbolic alteration may be found in Benjamin's cards in *The Sacred Tarot*.

We may examine three of these different packs, and note the effects of certain alterations: a comparison between the Marseille set, the Levi set, and the Waite set will illustrate some of the difficulties. In the Grimaud Marseille pack, we find that the Wheel of Fortune *atout* is a picture of a revolving, six-spoked wheel with one monkey or devil moving down on the circumference and one moving up, and a third, wearing a crown and bearing a sword, sits on a strange platform on top of the wheel (figure 270). This design corresponds to the simple image of the tenth Arcanum in its original form, though the earliest card (Visconti) shows the traditional mediaeval image of the wheel of fortune. Levi's design of the same Arcanum has changed this image completely. We have a different kind of wheel, the ascending and descending monkeys are now labelled *Azoth* and *Hyle*, both of which must be the personal interpretation of Levi. Neither *Azoth*, the Paracelsian universal healer, the alchemical name for Mercury, nor *Hyle*, the basic material of the universe, finds much correspondence in this image. The monkey resting on top of the wheel has been transformed into an Egyptian sphinx, labelled *Archée*, which in the ancient tradition is supposed to mean the 'immaterial principle which presides over the phenomena of life', and which is linked neither with Egyptian doctrine in general nor with the sphinx in particular. In alchemical terms the same *Archée* was derived from a Greek root by Basil Valentine, but again there is no connexion with a sphinx. Levi has also added

268. Waite's version of Wheel of Fortune.

269. An Italian version of The Wheel of Fortune.

270. The Marseille Wheel of Fortune.

---

* *'For the variations in the symbolism by which the designs have been affected, I alone am responsible', he writes in his typical manner of condescension.*

271. *A Hebrew Tree of Life the structure of which some cartomancers use as the basis for their formal pattern for interpretation.*

272. *The title page and frontispiece to 'Aliette's' influential eighteenth century book on the Tarot.*

273. *A nineteenth century version of a sixteenth century Tarot card.*

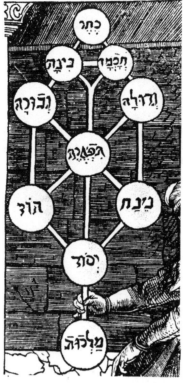

LA JUSTICE.

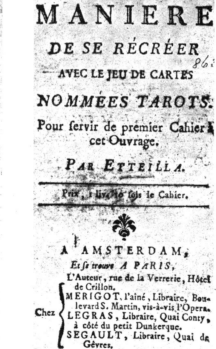

various other symbols which work to the same detriment of the symbol, by removing the Tarot from a hieroglyphic level to a semi-verbal description of a law in operation.

The Waite card goes one step further – the wheel is now a circle containing the name of God in Hebrew, the four characters interspersed with the four letter word *Rota*, a clumsy anagram of *Taro*, presumably made under the influence of Court de Gebelin. Inevitably, the sphinx is still there, balancing on top of the wheel, but the monkeys have disappeared, and we now have a snake, and an aardvark-like devil in human form. This amalgam of pseudo-Egyptian, Roman and personal imagery is surrounded by the Christian symbols of the four evangelists. Waite made no attempt to explain why he had departed from the original Tarot design, and why he incorporated so much rubbish in such an indifferent style: his promise of explanation, as made in his *Pictorial Key to the Tarot*, was never fulfilled.

This brief and random analysis indicates the dubious quality of the 'material' which has gone into the various accounts of the Tarot cards. The 'authorities' who have written about the Tarot cards appear as so many grinning Aunt Sallies, to be bowled over with a minimum of research. We find Court de Gebelin, who, in a sense, began it all towards the end of the eighteenth century and who is still quoted by some as an authority on the cards, claiming the Egyptian cards to be the remaining fragments of the libraries of the ancients miraculously preserved, and he appears to come to this conclusion by direct inspiration rather than by any other method. His ignorant assertions have lent an almost divine aura to the cards, and this malignant influence has persisted to this day. The curious Aliette, a perruquier-turned-cartomancer, transported the symbolism of the Tarot into the world of genii, talismans, dreams and fantasy, suggesting a fertile ground for some psychoanalyst. It is doubtful whether the Tarot will ever recover from the weight of his sterile verbiage – from his pen comes the finest piece of science fiction in this field, for in 1783 he seriously informed his readers that the Tarot was produced by seventeen Magi (one being a relative of Mercury) exactly 3,953 years previously.

Eliphas Levi may have been a brilliant *illuminé*, as some suggest, but his knowledge of history was more than casual, and his imagination dangerously strong. Still much quoted, in spite of his obvious lack of historical knowledge, he claims mighty things for the Tarot: it is very probably older than the Book of Enoch, it is a mystical summary of all ancient wisdom, it is the book of occult science, and it is (by some twist of mythology) the Book of Hermes.

Papus, perhaps the best known of the 'authorities', follows the dictates of Levi, and is a little more incomprehensible than the majority of writers: he has a charming way of revealing nothing behind a veil of obscure symbols. Waite, as we have seen, introduced his own peculiar symbolism into the pack, thus leaving the untying of the real knots to others, and presenting the world with a set of hints and guesses which scarcely even intrigue.

Ouspensky, who really should have known better, gives in superb language a very personal interpreta- of their meaning, mainly because he used in his meditation a pack which was not a genuine Tarot.

So much for the larger Aunt Sallies, though in fact the confusion is actually much greater than the comments above might suggest. The attempt of Papus and his like to link the names of Cardan, Lully, Postel and Saint Martin with the Tarot, creates an atmosphere of semi-desperation – methinks they all protest too much. Their vague and ineffectual attempts to introduce authorities into the history of the Tarot, on little or no evidence, has in fact rendered obscure that which is by its very nature obscure, and this has not helped the Tarot in any way. It is certain that if Tarot had been used in the early days as a system of divination or as a philosophical machine, then men as erudite and eager for such matters as Paraclesus, Fludd or Agrippa would certainly have included commentaries in their encyclopaedic works. The reading and study of the great number of books on the Tarot which have appeared in recent years is sadly unrewarding – even those who have somehow been accorded a reputation for explaining the cards, such as P. Christian, Rakoczi, Sadhu and the like, appear to be more inclined to gloss over the real knots of scholarship, than to spend time in the untying of them. Ill-deserved reputations abound nowadays, as much as in the past two hundred years.

The less said about the 'history' of the Tarot, then, the better: the Tarot has no history. On the other hand, this lack of history, like the collapse of all claims to glorious ancestry and famous antecedents, does not diminish the pack in any way. The force of the images, the computations of the philosophical considerations to which these remarkable cards give rise, the fact that such archetypal magic works as a divinatory method, and, indeed, the very quality of the cards themselves, all point to the greatness of the set, and suggests an obscure, esoteric but thoroughly beneficent origin.

273

The following list of books refers to titles and authors mentioned in the preceding text: there are very many books dealing with the Tarot, most of them extremely bad, many of them harmful, and it would be of little service to the reader to have a complete bibliography of the material.

BOULEAU C. *The Painter's Secret Geometry* (Eng. trans. Tiranti).

CIRLOT J. E. *A Dictionary of Symbols* Routledge and Kegan Paul.

COLLIN R. *The Theory of Celestial Influence* Stuart and Watkins.

CROWLEY A. *The Book of Thoth* Samuel Weiser.

D'AMBLY P. B. *Cartes a Jouer et la Cartomancie* (1859).

GEBELIN C. de *Le Monde Primitif Analysé* (Vol. VIII) (1781).

LÉVI Éliphaz *The Magical Ritual of the Sanctum Regnum* Thorson's.
La Clef des Grands Mystères (1861).

LHOTE J. M. *La Bibliothèque Volante* No. 1 April 1971.

MATHERS S. L. MacGregor *The Tarot: Its Occult Significance*.

MUCHERY G. *The Astrological Tarot*.

OUSPENSKY P. D. *A New Model of the Universe* Routledge and Kegan Paul.

PAPUS *The Tarot of the Bohemians* Wiltshire Publishing Inc.
Le Tarot Divinatoire (1909).

RAKOCZI B. I. *The Painted Caravan* Wehman Bros., Publishers.

VAN RENSEELAER J. K. *Prophetical, Educational and Playing Cards* (1912).

WIRTH O. *Le Symbolisme Hermétique* (1931).

WAITE A. E. *The Pictorial Key to the Tarot* Rider & Co.

I would like to thank the following individuals, galleries, photographers and institutes for pictorial material: The Arena Chapel, Padua (227); Baptistry, Florence (72); Bargello, Florence (30); Bibliotheque National, Paris (195, 222); Bodleian, Oxford (98); Brogl, photo (72); British Museum (9, 47, 51, 56, 67, 101, 102, 116, 123, 125, 139, 142, 148, 150–154, 160, 170, 236, 264, 266, 272); Camera Press (255, 256); Fitzwilliam Museum, Cambridge (53, 210, 235); Giraudon (204), Gropina, Italy (213, 216, 217); Michael Holford Library (43, 52, 89, 171, 253); Editions Houvet (90, 91); Keystone Press (10, 11); Jean Marie Lhote (176); Marvin Lichtner/Observer Camera Press (1); National Gallery, London (162, 189); Mansell Collection (159); Parma Gall. Nazionale (193); Fay Pomerance (198); Reims Cathedral, France (176); Scala (99, 104, 136, 193, 223); Scottish National Portrait Gallery (8); Scrovegni Palace (136); The Tate Gallery, London (178, 186, 188); Rodney Todd-White (35, 178, 186, 188); Uffizi, Florence (99); The Warburg Institute, London (43, 89, 171, 253). The various examples of the Waite cards were reproduced with the kind permission of Rider & Co. The various examples of eighteenth and nineteenth century Tarot cards were selected from the author's collection. The diagrams were drawn by Ann Dickie and the author, whilst the modern interpretation of the Marseille pack were prepared by John Hardy and the author. The photographs of the predictive methods of astrology, the *I Ching*, and cartomancy, were taken by the author.